Answers To: Where Do We Go From Here?

By Leroy Nelson
Foreword by Patrick Lockhart

Published in Portland, Oregon by
No Hate No Violence Press
https://nohatenoviolence.com

About the cover:
"The Eternal Butterfly"

We each walk our own path in life, and each life comes with many different steps and stages. The path we walk ultimately leads each of us into the light and then onward into a new life.

This image symbolizes the whole life experience – the path we all follow from before birth, through this life experience, then past the end of this life and on to a new life with fresh challenges and possibilities.

Dedication

To my forever bride, Carolyn (Brewer) Nelson, my three kids, Scott, DeAnne, and Gregg, plus my five grandchildren and one great- grandchild

The First Recorded NDE?

According to "Resuscitation Journal", many scholars have analyzed mystical and historical possible experiences of NDE in ancient civilizations. These include ancient records from Pharaonic Egypt, Mesopotamia, Vedic India, Greco-Roman Antiquity, pre-Buddhist China, Himalayan Buddhism, and pre-Columbian Meso-America. The Journal recently published an 18th century description (circa 1740) given by a physician, which appears to be the oldest Western professional medical case report of NDE. The author was Pierre-Jean du Monchaux (1733–1766), a military physician from Northern France.

"Sir L.C., one of the most famous apothecaries of Paris had in Italy, 25 years ago, a malign fever, and was treated by French physicians and surgeons, and sustained many blood-letters. After the last phlebotomy – which was very important – he had a syncope and was unconscious for such a long time that the assistants were particularly worried. He reported that after having lost all external sensations, he saw such a pure and extreme light that he thought he was in Heaven (literally: in the Kingdom of the Blessed). He remembered this sensation very well, and affirmed that never in all his life had he had a nicer moment."

According to the Journal, "…even if the data are limited, this 18th century patient report scores 12/32 using the Greyson criteria for assessing depth of NDE – whereas a total of more than 7/32 is considered a true positive NDE."
https://tinyurl.com/ygw579v9

Table of Contents

Foreword

THROUGHOUT LIFE, we're all faced
with the same existential questions that
author Leroy Nelson examines in his
thought-provoking book, *"Answers To:
Where Do We Go From Here?"*
I've had the privilege of enjoying 25
years of friendship with the author. I am
amazed at the incredible amount of
information he has managed to pack
into this well-organized read on a
subject we all wonder about. I am sure
this book will leave you feeling as good
as I did when I finished reading and
pondering the questions raised
throughout the book.
"Answers To: Where Do We Go From
Here" isn't written just for older adults;
the author's calm and thoughtful voice
speaks to everyone from their teen years
on up. People of all ages contemplate
but rarely discuss the important issues
that Nelson brings to light. Is there a

human spirit? If so, where does that spirit go when our bodies die? Is reincarnation real? Is there a Heaven and Hell? These are questions all of us wrestle with as we navigate life's ups and downs, its peaks and valleys, it's triumphs and defeats.

One thing remains the same though, namely, no one person has the right answer for everybody. Though most people follow one of the world religions, every one of us has our own unique beliefs. And those deep-seated beliefs (including our faith) will either provide us comfort or distress when our time to leave this world comes.

It's clear throughout Nelson's writing that his main goal is to get each reader to examine their own faith, to test their own beliefs, and to be comfortable in whatever views they have regarding death and what, if anything, follows after.

He eloquently and thoughtfully provides insights from different religions, different scientific and medical figures, and ordinary people who have experienced extraordinary circumstances. His casual, yet witty style of writing allows readers to participate in what feels like a late-night chat with a long-time friend. As such a friend, he wants to draw us out on a topic most of us tend to avoid – our own death. That's what friends do.

Lauren Pries, a former Director for nohatenoviolence.com, said that while reading this book she found herself fascinated not only by the incredible accounts of Near Death Experiences (NDE) but also found herself on a journey of looking introspectively and reflecting on a similar experience she once had. That's how this book affected me too – it helped me look inside and examine my life in light of what I already sort of knew but wasn't really looking at clearly.

It's clear that Nelson has put immense thought into writing something that provides both an opportunity to learn about the various schools of thought and an opportunity to work through ones' own feelings regarding death of the body and the extended prospects of one's spirit.

Inquisitive, intriguing, and stimulating on a relatable level – "a call to caring not only about our own death but about our family and dear friends".

Those words best describe this book for me, and I hope that you will experience the same joy, newly aroused curiosity, and sense of inspiration that I did after reading this deep-thinking author.

Patrick Lockhart, Founder
https://www.nohatenoviolence.com

Acknowledgments

THANK YOU TO MOUSE SCHWARTZ who, after he died, cared enough about me to alert me to the existence of a spirit world, which has inspired me to research and write about what has been debated for ages.

Thank you to my coaches and teachers for imparting their wisdom, guidance, and discipline so I would grow up and apply responsible foresight one day.

Thank you to Joe Moses who mentored me in basketball and life.

Thank you to Lauri Devine, who provided heartfelt and objective content editing.

Thank you to Pat Lockhart for his insightful and well-crafted foreword.

Thank you to Johnny Bench, for being the best catcher Major League Baseball has ever seen ... and a great friend.

Introduction

For every aspect of life, there are classes available to improve one's experience and lay the groundwork for future success. Classes to learn how to drive a car, birthing classes, parenting classes, classes on how to start and run a business, classes to teach trade and art skills. Some classes apply to nearly everybody, but most serve a limited and specific population.

Death applies to everyone, doesn't it? The statistics from all of history are in: There is a 100 percent mortality rate for all species! Yet, where are the classes on death and dying? How did this inevitable human experience get so swept away that there are few classes you can attend to better prepare for your death? Other than estate planning and insurance presentations, death has taken a back seat in Western consciousness, and ignorance is the reward for our collective apathy. Being ill prepared for the death of your friends and family, and for your own death, is the inevitable result.

There is a mystery attached to death, and with that mystery comes fear. Let's be honest; almost all of us fear death. And why not? Think of all the seminal moments in your life thus far: first pedaling a two-wheel bike or ice skating without holding onto someone, your first date, the initial attempt at driving a stick- shift vehicle, your wedding, the birth of your first child, putting that child on a school bus for the first time, or seeing your son or daughter off to college or to war.

There was an element of fear with each of those events. Why? Because they were all new experiences for us. They were unexplored emotional territories. You hope for the best but do not have control of the outcomes.

Why would death be any different? Is it a destination or a transitory part of the journey? This book is an honest attempt to give you a perspective about death that may enable you to approach it in a way that is tailored for you.

I have been investigating this topic for years. I haven't approached it with an agenda, other than to get empowered to face the end of life with more excitement than fear and more security than aimlessness. To aid you in this journey, it may be necessary for you to examine tough topics in an honest way. To do anything less would be selling yourself short. A ruthlessly honest personal inventory and exploration of sensitive issues is a necessary part of this journey. Where do we go from here? The answer to the question lies within your heart. Through examples of many lives, laughter, and tears, may this book help to guide your soul and mine.

—Chapter 1—
Death 101

> "Death is just life's next big adventure."
>
> J. K. Rowling b. 1965

THIS BOOK DARES TO ASK and (perhaps even more daringly) to answer questions about our existence now and about after we pass on and suggests what to do to prepare for the day of our own death. The stories told represent people who had experiences that made them rethink their philosophy of life. We can benefit from them. This is important. My hope is that those who are open, honest, and questioning and actually notice the events in their lives may rethink and change their ideas about some things after reading this book, and then may change their behavior to match.

This is neither a religious nor antireligious book. We are looking at life's penultimate question with an open mind.

Like the national news network slogan, I see my job as reporting what I've found; then asking you to decide. I've learned so much from the unique life experiences of others that I want to share what I've learned with you. You free to reconcile for yourself whether these undeniably powerful experiences are proof of an after-life or whether they simply raise more questions.

To question life after death has always been a part of the human experience. For many, the question was answered by devising gods (religious expressions), devising theories (philosophical expressions), or both, that gave an answer to the question: Where do we go from here?

I am assuming that your motive for reading this book is either to:

~ Further validate your existing views and understanding, or;

~ Recognize whatever gray areas you have about death, start with a clean slate, and look at facts and testimonies to build a new bridge of understanding. The girders that support that bridge are both rational and forged by faith. Yet, many say it can't be both. The age-old dichotomy has been:

Thesis = Faith	Antithesis = Logic

The philosophical missing link has been the synthesis – the middle ground. Could that be called logical faith? Beliefs based on rational factors and validated accounts?

Most academic teaching is – quite reasonably - centered on reason. Unfortunately, this means that students of all ages are forced to the opposite corners of faith or reason, like a boxing match. Nonetheless, many of the world's best doctors, scientists, inventors, composers, and even philosophers rejected that either/or paradigm and forged ahead in synthesis – Reason &

Faith- with brilliance and greatly benefitted mankind. If we look back to these great men and women of history, it begs the question: Why can't we? Why can't we enter the synthesis realm of faith and logic and see where it takes us? Before we embark on this journey, it is best to see what road to death you are on right now because you may need to change roads ... very soon!

Roads To Death

Religious Dogma - Most Of Humanity

Casual or devout adherence to traditional religious dogma

Philosophy & Reason - Much Of Humanity

Self-introspection & hoping for the best

Unbelief - Some Of Humanity

Don't care; prefer independence to immortality

True Religion - Few Of Humanity

Do care; Will serve the Creator (God) at all costs

—Chapter 2—
The Amazing Death of Mouse Schwartz

"The chain of destiny
can only be grasped
one link at a time"
Winston Churchill 1874 - 1965

Richard "Dick," AKA "Mouse," Schwartz (1935- 2002) and I were friends since 1939. He was adopted as a baby and never knew his birth parents. As a youngster, he was nicknamed by a YMCA worker called Hat. Dick was short for a sixth-grader, and thus Hat called him Mouse, and it stuck. (Schwartz subsequently grew to be six-foot one inch and a star on a state championship basketball team in junior college.) Because my last name is Nelson, I was given the nickname of "Nellie."

Mouse was a pretty religious guy. He was highly intelligent—an A student in high school and college. Years after Mouse retired from his career at Georgia-Pacific, he was diagnosed with cancer. His battle with it lasted about six months.

Near the end the disease had caused him to wither away to a fraction of his normal frame.

A short time later, Mouse died, around 1:00 a.m. At that time, my wife and I were sleeping at our home in California, some 1,400 miles away. At exactly 3:19 a.m., the clock alarm (atop our bedroom TV) went off for no reason. Neither of us had set it to go off. What made this amazing is that Mouse was born March 19, 1935 (3/19). After we were awakened at 3:19, we heard Mouse's voice say, "Nellie, don't worry about me. I'm fine." It was as if he was in the room with us! It wasn't a dream or hallucination because my wife Carolyn heard it too. She even recognized his voice.

It was this inexplicable experience that made me open to the real possibility that one's spirit existed after bodily death. How and why Mouse's spirit could, or would, make verbal contact with any human was beyond my comprehension. This book is born of the curiosity about that event. More than ever before I wanted to find answers to where we go from here.

"Forgive all your life issues, forgive everyone and everything in your life. Fear is the only hell," said the angel, "Love your life, everyone and everything, and fear no more."

At that very moment, I came face to face with my life and trusting in life as never before, I said and meant, "I love my life, all of it." I surrendered, and what an incredible release that was. Loving my life freed me from my hell. I felt free and light, the first inklings of a loved life.
Andrew Mellon-Thomas

—Chapter 3—
The Essence of Life

"We are not human beings
having a spiritual experience;
we are spiritual beings
having a human experience."
Pierre Teilhard de Chardin
1881-1955

WHAT MAKES YOU, YOU? Are you just a collection of bones, muscle, organs, tissues, blood, proteins, minerals, and gray matter? Or is there more to you than that?

I propose to you that we are a magnificent combination of spirit, soul, and body. In fact, the main thing about you and I is spirit. We are eternal spirits, in temporary communion with a soul (mind, will, emotions, conscience), sojourning in a tangible body. But don't take my word for it. I'm not a doctor, theologian, or philosopher. Let's see where others weigh in on this concept of humanity:

F. LaGard Smith (1944-) was a district

attorney in Oregon. Later, he became a law professor at Pepperdine University in Malibu, California. As a DA, he attended autopsies related to murder investigations. In one of his books. Out on a Broken Limb, he recounts how he felt at the first autopsy he attended. Since most of us will never be present at such a morbid event, we can benefit from his experience:

My greatest lesson about death came when, as a young District Attorney in Oregon, I watched an autopsy for the first time   In the middle of the room, occupying center stage, was the stainless-steel examining table. On it lay the stiffened body of a young man, about twenty-five years old. He and I were the same age.

That, alone, had a chilling effect on him. Smith continues:

"Now he is dead. And there we were brought together — not because of his life, but because of his death....

I could see the blue fingernails, the dried blood, the partially formed bruises, the slack mouth, the barely discernable stubble shadowing the body's puffy jaw   The morgue door opened, and [the coroner] Dr. Scott entered. Briskly and professionally gathering up his macabre tool his scalpel gleamed in the bright lights as he made his first incision."

[Dispensing with the disturbing details, let's focus on the DA's impressions.]

'I was fascinated with the intricacy, the complexity, [of] the muscles, veins, and organs. I was drawn (involuntarily) closer to this master machine. I wanted to see, up close, the secrets of human life. [Scott] enjoyed the role of a teacher, carefully explaining the function of each organ. I was most intrigued by his explanation of where the organs were placed. The most vital ones were in the best-protected areas and the others were nestled together in close companionship with the abdomen. The words of the Bible came back to me: We are

"fearfully and wonderfully made" [Psalm 139:14]

In death, there was little difference between a human body and any other body. I remembered how it was easier to call it "the body" than "the man." It struck me: This wasn't a man, but a shell. The man was gone.

But the most important lesson of the morning was yet to come. I was about to understand, for the first time, that the essence of a human is not material, but spiritual — that "me" was not equivalent to "my body" If someone had asked me, before this day, where my real person was located, I would have identified the mind or the brain (which seems to house the mind). After all, my thinking process harbors my innermost feelings. It is ... a matter of two different thinking processes— one more logical and rational, and the other more emotional and intuitive, but both inseparably tied up with thinking.

I knew for the first time, from experience, what (before) I had believed by faith: Who I

*am is not limited to my body. My
personality is not a by- product of my brain,
to die and decay like the rest of my body.
Who I am uses and expresses itself through
my body, but it is more than my body. My
body is only a part of me—not my essential
being. My emotions are not merely electrical
responses to stimuli but are more than that.
When I laugh, there is more involved than
just the electrical impulses of the brain—
telling my throat and lungs to work together
to make sounds associated with laughter.
When I cry, my tears are prompted by
something in addition to brain waves
It is the spirit part of the brain that matters.
Every gram of physical weight which this
man, on the autopsy table, had possessed
before death still lay there in front of me. He
still had every one of his organs and limbs.
But he wasn't there. What his body was
missing was not physical, not material, not
quantifiable in grams and centimeters. Just a
day before, this body had been a person—
with intelligence, feelings, and emotions—
not just a living, breathing physical*

organism. This corpse in front of me was a discarded, decaying shell. The person was no longer there."

District Attorney Smith experienced a great truth that morning in Oregon: Although the human body is wonderful, and the brain is a sophisticated organism, the spirit of human being is more than one's body, and the spirit is not bound to the body in death. On the contrary, it is the spirit that gives the body life, not the body that gives the spirit life. Death dramatizes, as nothing else can, the fact that the spirit leaves the body at death.

Years later, the DA's father died, and there was a family viewing at a funeral home. Smith's autopsy experience helped him face the personal decision of whether to look at his dad's corpse one last time. He chose not to and said he never regretted that decision. His father was more than the shell he recognized as his dad.

My view of death has been radically

altered by the autopsy experience. For weeks afterward, the lessons of the autopsy colored my thinking. I viewed the world in a new light. I concentrated on life's meaning and ultimate things. This book is a means for us to also take F. LaGard Smith's journey, to concentrate on "life's meaning and ultimate things," such as love, faith, hope, and service.

Smith concludes:

"We are human beings and that is wonder enough. Of far greater significance—and crucial to understanding what life is about—is the fact that we are, first and foremost, spiritual beings...."

As Aleksandr Solzhenitsyn observed, *"We are outraged if someone gives his soul as much attention as his grooming." But that's all backward. The truth is, that we are primarily spiritual beings within quite secondary physical bodies."*

In a 2013 article for *The Clearing,* entitled *"We Are Spiritual Beings Having a Human Experience,"* Betsy Koelzer (1962-), defines the term spiritual psychology:

"Spiritual Psychology is founded on the principle that we are each Spiritual Beings having a human experience. Sit with this statement for a moment and it becomes self-evident. We are not human beings striving to be Spiritual; we are already Spiritual Beings First and foremost, we are eternal Souls. In the very quiet moments of our busy lives we can re-connect with this knowledge."

She concludes:

"As Spiritual Beings, it is important for us to appreciate the value of learning and growing at the Soul level.... Earth is your school and the class is in session."

Though Mr. Smith, a law school professor, and Ms. Koelzer, a recovered drug addict and counselor, have extremely divergent views about spirituality, they do agree that we are, first and foremost, eternal souls (spiritual beings).

I end with an excerpt of Aleksandr Solzhenitsyn's 1978 Harvard University commencement address:

'If humanism were right in declaring that man is born only to be happy, he would not be born to die. Since his body is doomed to die, his task on earth evidently must be of a more spiritual nature.

It cannot be unrestrained enjoyment of everyday life. It cannot be the search for the best ways to obtain material goods and then cheerfully get the most of them.

It has to be the fulfillment of a permanent, earnest duty so that one's life journey may become an experience of moral growth, so that one may leave life a better human being than one started it."

—Chapter 4—
A Smorgasbord of Beliefs

Like most people, I wonder where our spirit goes when we die. Our physical body goes away, but our spiritual life seems to continue. How do I arrive at this conclusion? Many of the accounts that are shared in this book reveal that something else exists 'but there."

The religions of the world have set doctrines on death and the afterlife. According to Adherents, an independent, non-religiously affiliated organization that monitors the number and size of the world's religions there are over 4,200 religions around the globe.

Each has tried to answer: Where do we go from here? Many books already detail the beliefs of world religions, so we will focus on the death and after-life views of just the ten major religions.

As you study these dominant religions (which I define as having a minimum of ten million adherents), you can see similarities and differences.
Eschatology is branch of theology that studies the afterlife. Each religions view of life after death, and reward versus punishment, are summarized in my words in the graphic to follow. Any one priest, rabbi, or follower of any listed religion may take some exception to my summary but, I hope, not take offense. You will note there is a clear majority who hold to an after-life, followed by a group that doesn't know, and then a group that doesn't care. At this juncture, it is important that you identify with where you are (or are closest to being) on any of those ten summaries. That is the starting point on your bridge of understanding. Fair WARNING: When you are finished reading this, your

ending point may not resemble your starting point. New knowledge and contemplations may cause a shift in you. The major distinction between Western and Eastern religions seems to be whether we get one immutable soul (or some say spirit) for eternity or whether that soul gets recycled from lifetime to lifetime. This is a determination I am not able, or willing, to pontificate on. In the end, it would just be my opinion. There are no guarantees that I can give you. I wouldn't want it that way because I cannot die your death. Only you can die your death, so your opinion is the only one that matters.

The following graphic showing comparisons between religions is to help you recognize the breadcrumbs that lead to your path. You may still have questions after seeing the graphic. There are more bodies of evidence to consider, as we digest chapter by chapter.

BELIEF	ESCHATOLOGY
Agnosticism	The prefix "A" means "Without", and "Gnosis" means "Knowedge"; thus, when it comes to things we can't be sure of we should come to grips with a lifetime of "I don't know".
Atheism	Belief in an afterlife is a construct of primitive people and is not scientifically justifiable and, therefore, is anathema to men and women of intellect.
Buddhism	Life is a series of death and re-birth (reincarnation) events but that cycle can be stopped, or fulfilled, by Nirvana - liberation from earthly desires. Anatta is the belief that we do not have eternal souls.
Christianity	People are made in the image of God, who exists in three persons - Father, Son and Holy Spirit. Those who believe in Jesus & are baptized have their sins forgiven and will live eternally in Heaven after death. Hell is for the Unsaved.
Taoism	Death is a returning home that humankind ignorantly resists and sees the individual living on after death dissolved in the many creatures of the earth.
Hinduism	A person cannot achieve permanent happiness in this world, so they strive toward a better future through reincarnated life (Samsara) by creating good Karma. Bodies come and go; the soul is eternal.
Islam	Life continues after death in the form of spiritual and physical resurrection. The afterlife will be one of rewards and punishments that are commensurate with earthly conduct, leading one to Hell or Paradise.
Judism	There is resurrection of the dead to Gan Eden (Heaven) or to Sheol, or Genion, where souls are punished for a time, followed by destruction. When his baby died King David said "I shall go to him; he shall not return to me."
Native American	Varies by tribe; there is a universal understanding that there is a spirit world. Some hold that there are two souls; one that dies with the body and wanders on after a journey to places the person has been to in life.
Shinto	Everyone has an eternal soul, or spirit. After death the spirit travels to one of 3 places: Akamanohara (Heaven); Yomi (The Underworld); or Tokoyo (beyond the sea). At some point the spirit becomes a Kami, or diety.

Has your perspective been broadened? I hope so. My goal is to shed light on the subject. It is your responsibility to see what the light reveals. In the 1700s, Matthew Henry made the observation:

"There are none so blind as those who will not see." Such people are content to be stuck in a philosophical, academic, or religious rut.

Two things all people have in common: (1) we are all born into the human race on Earth, and (2) we will all die and leave Earth one day.

As we wrap our minds around these two simple, basic truths, it's easy to see that we are all in this together. Add to that our common human emotions of love, fear, hope, anger, and mental curiosity.

We are a unique blend of proteins, minerals, and gray matter. No species is like us in any meaningful way, so let's celebrate our brotherhood and sisterhood as we seek (in a finite continuum) the essence of the infinite. While we're seeking, let us traverse the difficult and less traveled road of pondering our pawns. Do you wonder what that may mean? Please read on!

—Chapter 5—
Pawns to Ponder

"All the world's a stage,
and all the men and women
are merely players."
William Shakespere

Let's look at our lives as a chessboard.
Your pieces on the board are your life,
and your opponent is death. When the
opponent says, "Checkmate," that
means you've checked out.

One of our greatest problems as players
is that we regard the existence of our
pawns too cheaply. They seem
expendable to us, but are they? Pawns
serve a limited role, but that doesn't
mean it isn't an important role. They

protect the other pieces that have better offensive and defensive capabilities. At the end of the day, all pieces serve to protect the life of the king (your life). With strategy, they can neutralize the attacks of the opposing king. That's what good chess players do.

In real life, pawns are the little things we do to ourselves that build up to big things. Big things can shorten our time on the chess board - our time on Earth - like eating junk food, carrying around anger, and not exercising. Then there are real big things that make us lose pawns at an unsustainable rate.

Professionals call them "High-Risk Lifestyles" and they include:

Serial alcohol consumption drug abuse (legal or illegal)

Smoking (legal or illegal)

Eating disorders Extreme sports

Self-mutilation

Criminal activities

Unsafe practices in the building trades

Distracted driving (texting, etc.)

Prostitution and casual sex
Constant exposure to EMFs
WiFi exposure
Microwaves radiation
Immoral or risky sexual activities

These things can hasten your death (either slowly or very quickly). For many of the above, expedited death is almost a certain outcome. For instance, a crack addict loses all his or her pawns and most, if not all, of the best pieces very quickly after beginning the crack game. Soon there are no defenses left and the crackhead's king is totally vulnerable to succumbing to the enemy's king death.

A different analogy is to envision a majestic throne as the embodiment of reality. As human subjects, we cannot force reality one way or the other. There can reign a hopelessness in us that our reality can never change, can never get better. Because it is so imposing, many prefer to run from reality by various means of escapism: alcohol and other drugs, movies, sex, sports, music, video gaming, TV viewing, being a workaholic, and other compulsive behaviors.

Truth is whatever our situation we either live within reality, live below it, or live above it.

A friend of mine is a leg amputee. Getting around on one leg is that persons reality and after it happened they had the same three choices we all have so often in our lives: live through it (just get by), live below it (let it ruin life), or live above it (by embracing technology, gutting through it, overcoming obstacles and stereotypes). It doesn't change the out- come (a missing limb), but it does change the individual's outlook! Constantly living

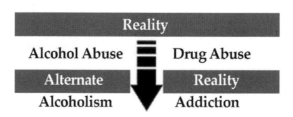

below (or above) reality results in an alternative reality.

Sadly, there are many examples of living beneath reality: Drug users and alcoholics tend to live below their reality. It is a distorted coping mechanism. The proof of the destruction of their pawns is high incidences of terminal disease and suicide. The solution?

Quit running from reality... stop ... turn around ... and run towards reality. Embrace it. Live wiser with new clarity and new freedom. A life of escapism only delays the inevitable. We escape from what we don't want to deal with. That is the prime motivation. However, if we choose to face those fears head-on now, we will be stronger for the next set of seemingly insurmountable challenges life may bring us in the future.

Is it easy to try to turn off entrenched habits and addictions? No way! That is why we need to have a support system to re-align with reality and cast-off thoughts of helplessness ... or even ending it all.

There are communities of support for the alcoholic, the drug addicted, the habitually battered, the depressed, the suicidal, the sexual abuser – for everyone fighting for their life. I've put contact information for a few that I know and trust in the Appendix & Resources section at the end of the book. Maybe you or a friend of yours is struggling to keep his or her pawns. See the appendix for various resources I've become aware of to help protect, and even regain, pawns in the game of life. There are people out there who have devoted their lives to helping folks with their toughest challenges and most painful memories. I encourage you to freely drink from the fountain of their love, compassion, and caring.

Why am I dumping all this on you? Because I care about your pawns. They are more valuable than you think; and YOU are more valuable than you can imagine. Let's be pro-reality as a means of truly living life before we go.

To live an addictive lifestyle is to be "realityphobic." Though it is manifestly more acceptable to cheer on those with a politically correct phobia or way of living, the likelihood of an accelerated end of life justifies lovingly telling the realityphobe that he or she is headed down an elective road to unnecessary destruction.

In the 1950s, a popular TV game show was called Truth or Consequences. There's even a town in New Mexico by that name. As a game show, it was fun to watch, but in life, if we don't live by the truth, we all have face the consequences. I implore you to commit to giving greater attention and more care to your pawns.

Non-acceptance has always been the life of those who deviate from norms – that is nature itself. Those loved ones who do not accept, say, binge drinking behavior do not hate the binge drinker, but they may hate the thought (or likelihood) of that person contracting cirrhosis of the liver or dying in a DUI car wreck. Thus, to accept your alternate reality is no less a way of saying: "I don't care if you get sick or hurt in a crash." How loving is that? Where is the love when it runs contrary to the medical statistics that are stacked against unnatural addictions and exploits like alcoholism and intravenous drug use?

"As the Being moved away from me I began to feel lighter. My pain and guilt lessened and I understood that I had been shown my deeds on Earth, not to harshly impugn me, but rather to lovingly instruct me.

Through the panoramic life review I had been given the knowledge of how to correct my life, and use my power of love to make a difference in the world. I was later told that human beings are powerful spiritual beings meant to create good on Earth, and that good starts with small acts of kindness."   *Dannion*

—Chapter 6—
Body - 0, Soul - 1

"I went to medical school because I wanted to ask big questions. Do we have a soul? Does God exist? What happens after death?"

Deepak Chopra b. 1946

WHAT HAPPENS WHEN WE DIE?
This chapter is a bit technical. For some, that will be fascinating, but others may find it morose. Still, it needs to be said, so we will all be on the same page.
When a person looks at death, there are two camps. You are either a fatalist or a futurist. Which one are you?
First, let's define clinical & legal death and what is biologically death:
In clinical death, the body stops breathing with no heart rate for up to six minutes. Clinical death is the precursor to biological death. Clinical death causes include, but are not limited to, hypothermia, suffocation, asphyxiation,

drowning, injuries, poisoning, and anaphylaxis (shock).

In biological death, the brain and organs are so deprived of oxygen that (internal) cellular death has taken place. Like clinical death, there is no breathing and heartbeat, but there is also no brain activity, and more time has/ passed, leading to cell death (organ degeneration) on a grand scale.

Remember I said there are two schools of thought?

Fatalists believe that death is finality. There is nothing else. Their view can be summed up by the Epicurean axiom: *"Eat, drink, and be merry, for tomorrow we die."* There are some ascetic fatalists too. They don't ascribe to lavish lifestyles as a measure of pleasure.

Futurists, in this context, believe that death is a beginning. There is much more to come. Their view is summed up by a quote from John Milton: *"Death is the golden key that opens the palace of eternity."*

For another perspective, we may look to Emily Dickinson:

"Because I could not stop for death, it kindly stopped for me; the carriage held but just ourselves and immortality."

The two positions have one similarity: that the body dies and becomes an empty shell that will eventually fertilize the soil it's placed in through decomposition or by cremains that are broadcasted. The irreconcilable difference is that the futurist expects the spirit/soul to find another (or better) resting place. It serves as a basis of hope and even motivation to live a positive and fulfilling life on Earth.

Many doctors and scientists believe that death is death, period. They talk about the shutting down of the body. When the arterial system is dead, so are you. They can't explain the fact that a spark still exists.

I lean towards believing that the spirit travels away to a new body. Here's why: Several accounts reveal that the spirit lives on. For example, Andy Anderson was an outstanding student in Iowa and a great athlete, excelling in football, basketball, and baseball. In 1943, he joined the navy and became a fighter pilot. He was based on a carrier in the Pacific fleet. On a fateful mission, Andy was shot down and presumed killed in action. About that time, a baby boy was born in Andy's Iowa hometown. As the boy grew, he looked just like Andy. Moreover, he exhibited the same athletic skills Andy had. People that knew both Andy and the boy said the kid was the spitting image of Andy. Some Iowans believed it was the return of Andy to live out his life that was cut short, albeit in a surrogate body.

Of course, this account can't be scientifically proved. Doubtless, the little Iowa boy did not have Andy's physical DNA, but I appreciate the irony... and would like to think that this is a way things can end up. I'm not saying it is the only way things end up.

Obviously, I am a futurist. Why? Because life's too short to be a fatalist. Indeed, a fatalist only looks to this life as his or her end-all. In my mind, fatalists are under more stress. It's as if they have to fit an eternity of existence into a measly eighty years or so (maybe much less). Oddly, the more stress they live under, the shorter (or more miserable) their life may be. This can result in what's called a Golem effect, namely, a negative self-fulfilling prophesy.

No small contributor to another stress Americans are under is our culture of death.

One Family's Story

"Help us! Help us!" Finally, a young doctor came and checked my sister. She briskly informed us, "Her heart is still beating, but it'll stop when it runs out of oxygen." Rage filled me. I wanted to scream, "How can you just let her die?!" ... Then, all at once, I could feel my sister's spirit.

Her energy was hovering in the room. In life, her love had always felt a certain way, it had

*a certain flavor. I felt it strongly now. It
replaced my anger with joy.*

*She told me, "I'm fine. I'm so wonderful!"
Rejoicing, she filled me, my brother, even the
doctor and nurse, with her love. She also
filled me with The Light again, which
reawakened in me memories of Its brilliance,
so much so that I struggled to conceal my
joy.*
Louisa Peck

—Chapter 7—
Cultures Of Death

"The hand that rocks the cradle
rules the world."
William Ross Wallace
1819-1881

IN HIS 1865 POEM, Wallace makes the point that whoever raises a child (and so, influences the young one's worldview and morality) influences the coming society of that baby's generation. Thus, the question for our day is: Who is really raising little Johnny? More and more, the most significant influencer of children is not Mom and Dad, not older siblings, not school teachers, or church attendance but television, movies, music, social media, and a plethora of engaging video games.

It is the latter that makes death and dying sanguine and acceptable. Psychiatrists note that although TV and movies show killings of various sorts, the child or adult is a passive viewer of these acts. However, with video games, when there is killing, the child or adult gamer is an active participant.

Studies estimate that the typical American child will view sixteen thousand murders and two hundred thousand acts of violence on TV by the time he or she graduates high school. Seriously? That would equate to 2.43 killings every day of his or her life. Now, of course, the child doesn't have it happen every day (unless he or she is a gamer), but just watching one war movie, like 12 Strong, will supply the viewer with two weeks' worth of killing ... thank you very much!

In our country's past, death was shocking, even horrifying. At the earliest American cinema venues, a normal audience would go to the movie theatre and attend, say, the premiere of a western film. When the cowboy shot the Indian, and the Indian died, some women would faint, others would scream or at least cry. Some men would leave the theatre. It was too much, too traumatizing to deal with in an entertainment setting. Life was so precious and sacred; the thought of viewing someone's death (even that of a stranger) for entertainment was morbid and unacceptable. But over time, the images just kept coming, and the reactions got duller and duller until there was no shock or horror at the sight of it.

The movie 12 Strong is a 2018 American war movie directed by Nicolai Fuglsig. It is based on the book "Horse Soldiers" by Doug Stanton.

Once that was achieved, there came exploitation of on-screen killing. It became expected that a revengeful death awaited every villain. The viewing public was no longer content to see the bad guy brought to justice in a jail. No ... he needed to be shot or hanged (still referring to Westerns).

Even children's cartoons became fraught

with death and acts of violence. It seemed innocuous that a two- ton rock would fall on the coyote character (Who was eternally chasing, and never catching the roadrunner). But then he would always show up again in the next scene. The finality of death was systematically removed from children's psyches by virtue of redundant killings without consequence (or blood). When their character in a game gets killed, the gamers can respawn and continue playing. Out of that, two problems arose: (1) they lost the ability to grasp the gravity and finality of death on this Earth, and (2) these kids grew up to run our society today.

To accommodate these maturing miscreants of death (meaning humans detached from death's realities), the entertainment industry had to go to greater (or baser) images to keep the public's (now insatiable) appetite for death intact.

First, it was simply more deaths, but that

lasted only for a while. Next, there were either more gruesome deaths or killing characters the audience developed an emotional attachment to. Hollywood realized that the death of, say. Old Yeller had more of an impact on some theatre-goers than seeing a dozen Indians shot off their horses by the cavalry. Just sayin'.

Because I was a teacher for years, how about a fun little pop quiz?

What do the following movies have in common? Chronicles of Narnia, Indiana Jones-Kingdom of the Crystal Skull, Kill Bill, and The Outlaw Josey Wales Answer: They each feature a minimum of seventy-five deaths! The three most-recent high body-count movies portray over 2,500 kills. Who has time for a plot?

Death Events by Film Genre			
Animation		Romance	
Akira	119	The Titanic	307
American Pop	61	True Lies	71
Transformers: The Movie	47	Atonement	34
The Incredibles	16	Slumdog Millionaire	8
Science Fiction		Comedy	
Starship Troopers	256	Kelly's Heroes	139
Equilibrium	236	Versus	127
Chronicles of Riddick	187	From Dusk To Dawn	122
Dune	186	Hot Shots! Part Deux	114

These numbers avoid the higher death genres like horror, war, crime, and Westerns. Excuse me . . over one hundred kills in comedy movies? Sheesh!

The mass desensitization of death over the last four generations has produced a culture of death. It has seen a cultish rise in death-centric groups, like the Hemlock Society, now called Final Exit. Consequently, in 1994, Oregon became the first state to legalize physician-assisted suicide. I merely touch on that because we are focusing on pathways after death, not methods to die.

Finally, the culture of death is fueled by a popularity in Satanism and matters of the occult that dwell on death.

On May 18, 2018, a sixty-two-year old private investigator in North Carolina went to a Sunday dinner with his family. He excused himself from the table, went out to the parking lot, and then drove his SUV right into the wall where their table was. He killed his twenty-six-year-old daughter and his daughter-in-law, left his wife and son in critical condition, and injured his   thirteen-year-old granddaughter.

The man's brother told reporters, *"The demons deep inside got the best of him and brought out the worst."* The very same day, an ex-Playboy model and her seven-year-old son checked into a Manhattan hotel. Their room was on the twenty-third floor. Later, she (with the boy in her grasp) jumped off the balcony, and they fell twenty-three floors to their death.

Just days ago (as of writing this

manuscript), a seventeen-year-old Texas youth arrived at his high school with a .38 revolver and a sawed-off shotgun. Minutes later, ten people were killed by his armed assault. He was wearing a trench coat (in May, mind you), and on the lapel of that coat was a satanic symbol. Also, the tee shirt he wore had three words on it: "Born To Kill."

Only weeks prior, a nineteen-year-old Floridian went to his former high school and committed mass murder. Twelve students and teachers were killed, along with five outside the school.

This is the kind of behavior a death culture foments. It's not limited to Satanism, jihadists, or racial supremacist groups. Evil is evil, wherever evil is. The issue is not the mode of killing but the culture of death that promotes these atrocities. This culture produces depraved hearts.

In states across America, a second-degree murder offense is called "depraved heart murder" or "depraved indifference." The legal definition of depraved heart murder is (in part): "killing someone in a way that demonstrates a callous disregard for the value of human life." Having seen depictions of two hundred thousand acts of violence by the time a child turns eighteen, it's a wonder all of them don't enter high school with a callous disregard for the value of human life.

So how do we process all these factors in our personal lives? This book can define the roles music, TV, movies, and gaming has had in desensitizing us, but are we left with enough humanity to cope with all this? What is the antidote to living in a culture of death?

Like anything that darkens our psyche or conscience, we can treat our desensitization to death as we would our bodies taking in too many bad things and go on a diet. That is, we can separate ourselves from influences that promote the death culture in us. What that looks like is, perhaps, a combination of; not listening to death lyrics, not viewing movies that bombard us with death scenes, not playing shoot 'em up video games, and not watching TV programs that obsess on death and dying. Whether it is a rerun of Murder She Wrote or Psych, there will be at least one death depicted on the show. We know that going into it. Choose to avoid it!

Perhaps we need to divorce ourselves from the death culture and make a commitment to surrounding ourselves with positive and life-giving music, movies and games. Maybe such a certificate would look like this.

CERTIFICATE OF
DEATH   DIVORCE

The bearer of this certificate makes
the following commitments:

I WILL think and say things
that are life-giving

I WILL avoid watching movie or
gaming death events

I WILL stop obsessive fears of
my or another's death

I WILL be quick to forgive those
who offend me

I WILL show appreciation for life
in big and small ways

*The benefits of the covenents above
are conditional upon the acts,
thoughts and words of the
bearer of this certificate*

DEATH HANG-UPS
ARE HEREBY DISSOLVED

What have we left out? Books. Many books entertain with characters killing other characters: murder mysteries, superhero comic books, etc.

Certainly, you have already read that characters we may love or sympathize with get killed in books.

Some examples are Lennie's death in the John Steinbeck (1902 - 1968) classic "Of Mice and Men".

Then there's Nancy, the girlfriend of the villain in Charles Dickens's (1812 - 1870) classic "Oliver Twist".

Also William Shakespeare (1564- 1616) Lavinia and Desdemona in "Titus Andronicus" and "Othello", respectively.

Of course George Orwell's (1903-1950) plot in "Animal Farm" called for the horse hero. Boxer, to be slaughtered.

Two key figures die in F. Scott Fitzgerald's (1903-1950) "The Great Gatsby".

The wrongful death of a black man brings a sad finality to Harper Lee's

(1926-2018) "To Kill a Mockingbird".
The list goes on, with the likes of J. R.
R. Tolkien, Leo Tolstoy, Stephen King,
Victor Hugo, J. K. Rowling, Oscar Wilde,
Mark Twain, Agatha Christie, Edgar
Allan Poe, Herman Melville, Truman
Capote You get the point.

Singers sing and poets write eloquently
of death. In 2001, the Beatles icons Paul
McCartney (1942-) and Ringo Starr
(1940-) visited a California dying man in
his seventies. It was former Beatle
George Harrison (1943-2001). Expecting
a languid, sullen, and lifeless Harrison,
they were surprised to hear him joking,
laughing, and pleasantly talking about
their heydays. This event (plus an Irish
woman who once wished Paul "a good
death") caused McCartney to rethink his
dim view of death and how he wanted
loved ones to process his passing
someday. His thoughts led to this
memorable song. See if you can tell from
these words whether McCartney a
fatalist or a futurist.

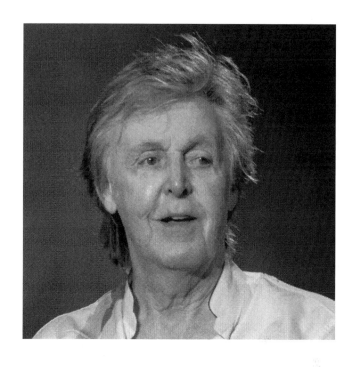

The End of the End
Paul McCartney

At the end of the end
It's the start of a journey
To a much better place
And this wasn't bad
So a much better place
Would have to be special
No need to be sad

65

On the day that I die
I'd like jokes to be told
And stories of old
to be rolled out like carpets
That children have played on
And laid on while listening to
 stories of old

At the end of the end
It's the start of a journey
To a much better place
And a much better place
Would have to be special
No reason to cry

On the day that I die I'd like
bells to be rung
And songs that were sung to be
hung out like blankets
That lovers have played on
And laid on while listening to songs
that were sung

At the end of the end

It's the start of a journey
To a much better place
And a much better place
Would have to be special
No reason to cry
No need to be sad
At the end of the end

"I reached out emotionally for the angel. I could see millions of souls still trapped in their private hells. Most of them were totally consumed by the traumas they had suffered or created in their lives. A few, from what I could see, seemed to actually be enjoying hell. Some others seemed to be bored with the whole thing. But millions of souls were begging to be saved. I asked why these souls were unable to be free.

"They are already free," answered the angel, "They hold themselves to negative patterns, memories, prejudices and fear."
Mellon-Thomas Benedict

-Chapter 8-

The Gambler

"Women's total instinct
for gambling is satisfied
by marriage."

Gloria Steinem b. 1934

I'm a gambler. There. I said it. This is not
meant to be a confession, just sharing a
hobby that Leroy Nelson has enjoyed
over the years. Maybe that's why
gambling didn't make the list of
destructive habits that take our pawns
away. Not just because it is something I
enjoy doing as a hobby but because
there are two kinds of gamblers: those
who risk bill money to keep gambling (a
foolish lot) and those, like myself, who
sensibly set limits and only gamble
excess play money (an eccentric lot). A
very small group of people can make a
living at it, and I know I am not one of
those people.

When you are wealthy, belong to at least
one country club, and are successful in

business, technology, music, or sports, you have play money, and that is the only money you should gamble with. To do otherwise is to guarantee more stress in your life. When I gamble, there are no piggy banks broken and no feelings hurt if I have a bad day. Why? Because I set a limit as to how bad a bad day can get. A low limit. It is a necessary form of self-control.

My most favorite challenge is poker, Omaha, specifically. It is a high/low game where the best hand and the worst hand share the pot equally.

Another hobby I enjoy is playing rounds of golf. To make that more interesting, I used to gamble on the course with the rest of the foursome. Putting money behind my shots motivated me to do better. Remember getting a quarter for every A on your report card? It's kind of like that. I viewed it as a form of golf lessons. Sometimes I got paid to take those lessons, but sometimes the lessons cost me two hundred dollars for eighteen holes.

Could've hired Lee Trevino for that much!

Years ago, my friend Dale Whiteside (1935-1988) once said to me:

"Leroy, you're a gambler, right?"

"Of course," I replied.

"Then why are you not hedging life's biggest bet?"

"What do you mean 'life's biggest bet'?" I asked.

"Life's biggest gamble is all about your eternity. If Jesus is right about being the Son of God and the only way to the Father in Heaven, then we would be foolish not to bet our lives on Him. If He's wrong, you've lost nothing in following Him, but if He's right, you'll lose everything for all eternity So why not hedge your bet and follow Him?"

(I am still thinking that one over.)

Dale was a good man, and I'll never forget that conversation. Why? Because he cared. Even if I don't share the same convictions as Dale, the language of caring crosses many barriers.

"'I've been watching you a long-time son and you have made many mistakes. Do you know where you are?' I looked around and replied, 'I'm not sure.' He said, 'You are death.' I looked around and panicked. He said, 'You scared.' I answered, 'No, I am not.' He then said, 'You've always feared this for no reason then.' I shook my head in agreement.

Next, he asked me, 'Do you feel in control?' I said, 'No, I do not.' He said, 'You've never had control in anything in your life. It's a veil or facade. You controlled everything in your life and it ultimately was wrong. I shook my head again and said, 'Yes, you are right.' He then said, 'You are be given a choice that many don't have. God is giving you the choice of going back and fixing the wrongs in your life or you can go through the gate.

However, you need to listen and heed these warnings. First, if you go through this gate

all of your regrets in life will torment your soul until you are given another chance. It will feel like an eternity.'"
William

Chapter 9

Near Death Experience (NDE) Stories

"For death is no more than turning us over from time to eternity."

William Penn 1644 - 1718

I'm sure you've noticed the great variety in the NDE stories I've shared with you so far. I find these accounts fascinating, in part, because I haven't had an NDE ... yet. Maybe you have! Nevertheless, doctors, lawyers, scientists, and psychologists have been fascinated by these phenomena for decades.

Before we go too far down this road, let's look at an analogy: No human was born capable of flying. It simply isn't in our DNA or RNA to be physically capable of flight. Yet every reader of this book has likely flown before. That is, you left the surface of the Earth. For a time, you were in another sphere, but you returned to your sphere.

A friend of mine was flying from Phoenix, Arizona (PHX), to Portland, Oregon (PDX), with his little boy. It was his four-year-old's first time to fly. The dad let his son sit at the window and gently explained to the boy each step of the process to ease any fears he might have. As they were taking off, he told the boy to swallow a few times to pop his ears (because the pressure was changing).

He explained that they would fly at an upward angle at first and then level off. When that happened, the boy suspected that his dad knew everything.

Next, he explained that they were heading west and that they would have to bank to the right to point the Boeing 747 to the north. Sure enough, the plane banked right, and now the boy knew his dad knew everything. However, the plane kept banking right... and dad was confused. Just then, the pilot came on and announced to the passengers that they were returning to PHX as a safety precaution. Sure enough, they soon landed back at Sky Harbor International airport in Phoenix.

Thus, the boy's experience was like an NDE. He left his realm (Earth) for the first time and returned where he came from. It was not his time to fly to Portland (at least not in that plane), and he was powerless to not go back. Yet he could say that he had experienced flight in the other realm ... for a few moments at least. NDEs are like that. They get to fly and maybe even land at their destination, but it is a forced round trip, and their destination is, in fact, a short layover till they can possibly stay the next time they come.

Between you and me, I don't appreciate the term "near death experience" because it seems to diminish the depth of the event. When your heart stops beating, you're not breathing, you have no brain waves: guess what? You're DEAD . . . not near dead, but dead! So, I regard NDEs as temporary or interim death experiences (IDEs). Perhaps they are just as providential as they are provisional; a test run, if you will. In 2014, scientists hoping to get a glimpse behind the final curtain, launched the world's most comprehensive study of human near death experiences, called AWARE. It is short for Awareness during Resuscitation.

Medical researchers spent three years interviewing and evaluating 1,500 patients who returned from the brink of death.

https://www.ncbi.nlm.nih.gov/pubmed/2 5301715

The key standard of observation was to place a picture on high shelves in operating rooms. The pictures could only be seen from an elevated vantage point. The litmus test was whether patients could describe the pictures without seeing them from the vantage point of the gurney or operating table. Such was the metric of proving that their out-of-body experience (OBE) was real and valid, simply put, that a person's spirit (with powers of observation and memory) could leave the body and return with recall of what he or she observed in that state.

Out of 1,500 patients, not one described a picture left on high shelves. One explanation for that was the inability of the researchers to control where the cardiac arrest took place. Thus, many were treated in rooms that did not have the designated items in place.

The whole thing came down to one patient who gave an anecdotal account of some phenomenon he or she experienced. The study was a flop. Before you insert a mental LOL right here, I must share that the pathetic response (1 out of 1,500) was, in part, due to their strict controls and required intensive interviews.

Moreover, I believe it was doomed from the start, based on human nature. For instance, let's say you are standing on a street corner downtown, and you hear an alarm go off from a bank building on the opposite corner. You look in that direction, see a man with a bag rush out of the building, and hop into a waiting SUV (with no other passengers). You observed the man was white, in his thirties, wore a knit cap on his head with brown hair sticking out on his forehead. You saw he had a brown goatee and noted that the SUV drove west on Main Street.

Later, the police interview you, and you share all the details you saw and remembered. Soon after, they catch the bank robber, and at trial, you are the state's witness to the crime. You convincingly tell the jury all that you saw (and remembered). However, on cross- examination, the defendant's attorney asks you if there was a sign on the glass door of the bank. You honestly say that you don't remember seeing a sign. With a gleeful smile, the attorney announces to the jury that, earlier that

Friday morning, a letter-size paper was pasted on the door to let customers know the bank would be closed the following Monday for a legal holiday. Because, you didn't see (or remember) the paper on the door, does that invalidate all the rest of your experiential testimony that day?

Hell, no.

Such was the problem with the AWARE research project. The pictures placed on high shelves were of no more consequence to these cardiac patients than the perfunctory notice on the bank door. Their attention was on the operating table. Most were struggling to reconcile that it was their body the medical staff was working on. Isn't it enough that these patients accurately describe the physical features of the doctors and nurses? That they can repeat (word for word) what was said while they were flatlined? Those are the things that matter; all the rest are meaningless details.

Other books and articles hail this research experiment as providing a smoking gun to out-of-body experiences. It doesn't, and anyone who says otherwise is being intellectually dishonest with you. Asking these patients to describe a random object on high shelves (during their OBE) is like asking you to look for a sand dollar in a diamond mine. Why would you?

In the medical world, many patients that revealed their NDE/OBE to their doctors were considered delusional. However, the recollections (from so many different ages and groups) were so similar the medical community could no longer afford to be dismissive of these accounts. In 2017, a study was conducted using 154 participants. All were identified as having an NDE. This was conducted on the campus of the University of Liège and its hospital in Belgium. The mission of the research was to determine "whether NDE features follow a fixed order or distribution," according to researcher Charlotte Martial. The published report is *"Temporality of Features in Near-Death Experience Narratives" in Frontiers in Human Neuroscience"*

What are NDE features? The following graphic illustrates the most common features and how frequently the participants encountered them. It is not an exclusive list; it includes just the most recurring features.

2017 NDE Research SOURCE; Frontiers in Human Neuroscience University (& Hospital) of Liège, Belgium

Name	M/F	Saw Light?	Feelings	Fought Return?	Saw Diety?	New Peace?
Taylor	F	Colors	Euphoric	No	No	Yes
Keith	M/F	Brilliant	Warm & Loving	No	Jesus	Yes
Richard	M/F	Bright	Peaceful	No	No	Yes
James	M/F	Bright	None	No	Jesus	???
Missy	F	Ye	Peace & Beauty	Yes	Jesus	Yes
Patricia	F	No	None	No	No	No
Alejandra	F	Yes	Extreme Happiness	No	No	Yes
Heidi	F	Golden	Peace & Love	Yes	Jesus	Yes
Dean	M	Flashes	Total Relief	No	No	Yes
Zdenka	F	Bright	None	No	No	???

Rounding out these documented NDE features are heightened senses, altered sense of time, extra-sensory perception, entering "the light," seeing one's life flash by, a feeling of harmony, accelerated thoughts, and futuristic visions.

One possible physiological explanation for seven out of ten people seeing a bright light is simply the brain slowly losing connections with the nerves that supply input, causing a neurological white out. The same would be true for the visual cortex if the eyes were no longer transmitting information. Yet it is anecdotally perceived (by many) as a portal to the celestial. Larry Dossey, MD (1940-) has studied NDEs and opines: *"The lack of fear, the dissipation of fear, the lack of terror, is something that… near death experiences are therapy for. In my experiences as a physician, I happen to believe the fear of death (and total annihilation with physical death) has caused more suffering, in the human race, than all the wars in history."* The 12 Most Common After-Death Communications

1. Sensing their presence while awake
2. Hearing their voice while awake
3. Feeling their touch while awake
4. Smelling their fragrance while awake
5. Seeing their apparition while awake
6. Seeing a flat vision of them like a photo while awake
7. Experiencing any one of these while half-asleep
8. Having a visitation dream
9. Having an out-of-body experience and meeting them

10. Receiving a telephone call (two- way conversations have actually been reported)
11. Experiencing physical activity such as lights, TVs, and radios going off and on.
12. Familiar objects appearing and disappearing in unusual places.

Let's take in some accounts of NDEs, as told by those who experienced them: Taylor nearly died of head trauma from a car accident at age fourteen. In her words:

"I was just a teenager, being stupid while drinking and driving with my older friends. Then I got tunnel-vision. It was dark and sparkly while my ability to see anything disappeared....

... Suddenly, my vision was back and in full HD [hi- definition] color. I can't describe the colors because I've never seen them before. I was somewhere else, completely unearthly. It was so incredible that I struggle to put it into words....

The best I can describe it is two giant skies or

atmospheres, split into two halves, like a split screen image with one sky on my left and the other on my right with a line down the middle separating them. Both sides were full of color.

It was very galaxy-like and spacey. The left had bright, sunny colors like yellow, light blue, white, and soft wispy cloud-like things everywhere. The right had darker colors, but not in a bad way. They were like deep sunset colors of red, gold, burnt orange, dark purple and black. Almost like a dawn on the left and dusk on the right. And in the middle of the right side was a tall thin white structure like a column or pedestal that went so high I couldn't see the top.

I never detected other people or Beings there with me. I was alone, with the urge to go on forward. I wasn't in a body, but was just floating or suspended.

The craziest part for me was the feeling of overwhelming euphoria. I didn't feel foggy or messed up in the head. I felt extremely clear, conscious, and happy. I felt so happy that it freaks me out to remember it.... After a moment. My hearing returned. I could hear my friend Jessica's voice and other voices shouting. Only then did it occur to me that "Oh yeah, I have a body in that other place right now.

Man, I really like it here though. I don't know if [I want] to go back. This feels so good here. Then thoughts about my life entered my vision. I saw my mom's face and I thought she'll be really sad if I stay here. She won't understand how amazing this place is. I never actually thought of it as "this is life after death." It was just, my body is over there somewhere, and I am here.

... I casually thought to myself, "ya know, I can't leave like this. I don't want them to worry, so I guess I should go back. Calm down everyone. I'm comin I'm comin". Then I instantly saw concrete, and hands on me. I saw my shirt and bra cut off next to me. I couldn't move or speak, so I was just stuck in my head for a few minutes watching them drive me in the ambulance and try to stabilize me. I was completely paralyzed but could see and hear.

. . . I've never been religious really, but that single experience is the only thing that makes me think maybe, just maybe, there is something after death. And if so, it's a very happy place. But I've never come anywhere close to experiencing anything like it again."
Keith was a young man who had taken LSD the day before. He woke up sick and partially blind. His mom took him to a doctor, who sent him to a hospital where he was placed in ICU.

While in ICU, my blood pressure went as high as 180/210. The doctors and nurses were frantically attempting to lower my Blood Pressure. I do not know the exact time my incident happened. I think it [was] in the late afternoon of the first day.

I remember leaving my body and rising up to the ceiling of the room. I saw the whole room and everyone working on me from the ceiling of the room. I was watching the heart monitor machine and saw that my heart had flat- lined. I saw that the hospital staff were trying to get my heart to start again.

Then I went into a winding, curving tunnel.

I felt no pain, only complete calmness. My whole life passed by me while I was traveling down this tunnel. It went very rapidly at first. Then some moments were slowed down. Every- thing was being shown to me; everyone I helped and everyone I hurt. Then a small pinhole light appeared at the end of the tunnel. As I got closer to it, the light got bigger and bigger. It was a brilliant white color, but not blinding. There was a warm, loving feeling coming from it.

I could not make out what it was though. As I got closer to the light, a figure of a person started to emerge. The closer I got, the clearer the image got. It was Jesus Christ. As I got to the end of the tunnel, I was stopped by Jesus, who said: "It's not your time." Then he reached his hand out and pushed me back to Earth.

I was back in my body. My heart was beating and I could sense the doctors were all relieved, but I cannot remember much after that point. My sight came back on the third day in the hospital."

Richard had the most recent NDE in this

book – the summer of 2017. While working at his farm, he fell off a ladder and suffered ruptured ligaments and tendons. Because he had Gilbert's syndrome, there were limitations as to what medications he could safely take. The hospital staff gave him a shot that was not appropriate for people with Gilbert's syndrome.

About 90 minutes after the injection I still could not stand. It took two people to get me out of the car and back to the family farm. I remember telling my sister that I didn't feel right.

I felt like I was flying. I looked at my left hand, thumb and index finger. My body was surrounded by an electrical blue force. As I tried to touch my two fingers, I felt them touch but they were one inch away from each other. I told my sister I didn't want to die and that I was floating away.

I remember seeing the treetops, located along the north fence line. I took one last breath, exhale [d] and I was over the treetops into total darkness! Everything was black, but I was floating. I could hear my sisters' voices, but the farther I floated away from them, the fainter their voices got.

Then I went from total black darkness to a bright white light. I was surrounded by clouds that seemed to be unfolding from the center of the light. I felt no pain. I felt an unending love and a sense of peace as I kept floating towards the light. At this point I couldn't hear my sisters. Then I heard a voice say, "It's not your time!" Then I was pushed back into the totally black darkness. I could hear my sisters' voices getting louder and louder.

Then WHAM! I was back in my body!

One of my sisters had slapped my right cheek so hard she left a red mark on my face. I gasped for air as I saw her face. I saw the emergency medical technician's face, and the EMT said, "We have him!" They said I was in full seizure mode for 20-30 seconds. I was gone for 10-15 seconds with no breathing and very faint pulse, if any.

... What I have trouble with, is dealing with the voice that said, "It's not your time!" I

don't yet understand the time issue. What is "time" in relation to the here and now when compared to the relation of "time" in the white light? I was dead for 10-15 seconds, in full seizure for 20-30 seconds, but it seemed like a flash in time. How did I go from seeing the blue energy haze around my left hand and two fingers, with everything in front of my eyes; all the trees, my sisters' voices, sights and sounds to nothing? I went to total black darkness, void of any light.

Then flash. I'm continually floating forward to the bright light surrounded by clouds without any indication of life in the clouds or life here on earth. I couldn't hear my sisters' voices anymore.

While gone, I had no pain from my fall off the ladder or any pain in my back, neck or my lower left leg. I had no pain. I wasn't sick anymore, I was floating. I don't know how to express this, but I was floating and moving forward. I was floating but it wasn't my physical damaged body, I left behind, which was a shell of who I am. There was something from inside me that was floating

91

away, and heading towards the light."
James C. was in a head-on car accident
in 1983. The collision sent him through
the windshield and out into the
elements. We pick up his story (which
he kept secret for twenty years) at the
point where he was lying unconscious
on the ground.
*"Before waking up, I remember seeing the
brightest white cloud you could ever
imagine.*
*In the center of the cloud was an image of the
face of Jesus. He told me, "It's not time yet."*
*After that, I instantly woke up to chaos and
confusion due to the loud sounds of
ambulances and police cars.*
*My head hurt tremendously, and I couldn't
see straight because of the concussion.*
*I always remembered, vividly, that
experience and (without a doubt) know that
it was real.*
*I am further emboldened by the fact that
others were told, "It's not your time yet" in
their near-death experience."*
Missy M., a mother of two, was in

surgery in 2016 under general anesthesia and experienced clinical death due to hypothermia.

"I suddenly awoke. I was not in a dream state but fully aware of where I was. I was standing in a desert-type area that was golden and hazy. I was standing on the edge of heaven. I looked at what appeared to be a wall. It looked like the walls surrounding an earthly city, but I knew exactly where I was, and that it wasn't earth or a dream. I was completely lucid.

The gold and blue colors I saw in the experience [are] indescribable; like a turquoise color mixed with the bluest hues of the ocean and intertwined with gold. It was the most magnificent thing I have ever seen and more importantly, I felt it. I stood there for what felt like forever.

I felt no pain, worry or fear. I had no feeling of "looking back." During this time, I never thought of my children because I had no thought of anything other than about peace and beauty.

I saw a person off in the distance, yet the

presence was all around me. It was Jesus and God at the same time, enveloping me in a feeling of love and peace; a love and peace that just didn't exist until that point.

... I suddenly had a thought or a feeling of want. I wanted to go inside the city. In a conscious thought I was about to take a step, when my deceased father and grandmother both said to me, "It's not your time, not yet. You have to go back." I could see and hear them both in one voice and in their own voices together. It is hard to explain that one in earthly language. I said, "No, I want to stay here with you." They each placed a hand on my shoulder and I looked into the eyes of Christ for a brief moment as he was suddenly there. He was not saying, but instilling in me, the thought that "everything will be okay" and a feeling of "we will meet again soon."

Suddenly, I was awake on the operating table. I know I was talking, because the nurse said to me, "I believe you, you're not the first to say things like that. I believe you." She continued to reassure me as I began to cry, realizing I was back in this miserable earthly life. The nurse wiped my tears and continued to reassure me.

I just cried and kept saying, "I want to go back. I don't want to be here." She then asked me if I had children. Suddenly, I wanted to be here again.

The feeling of peace, love, and beauty, had made me forget my two boys, ages 23 and 16 at the time. I knew then why I had to come back and continue living, yet I also knew of the beauty waiting for me. It is so profound. I know that I can get through anything to get back there to Heaven. This short narrative doesn't even come close to explaining my experience. There are not words to describe it, only the knowledge of knowing Heaven is real and I can't wait to go back when it is my time."

Patricia G. was clinically dead in 1980 in a hospital in Greece. She had an ectopic pregnancy and a tube burst, causing her to bleed out. She describes her NDE:

"I was above myself and high up in the rafters staring down at the hustle and bustle

going on below me. I could see them poking, prodding, and examining me. I listened as they said, "She's gone."

It was late at night and the attending doctor didn't have the necessary signing authority for the time-of-death certificate. They called for an authorized person to sign. I watched as my body was wiped off with some of the gore as everyone else stood quietly waiting. I think about 15 minutes passed. Then a woman with red hair entered.

She took up the chart and said, "She is too young. Let's try something else."

I was unaware of anything after that except that it was freezing cold. I woke up 4 days later. When I asked about the redhaired woman, everybody got very antsy. They said I couldn't have seen her because at that stage I was dead. The death part of the process is no more interesting than understanding one must first cook a meal before it's eaten."

Alejandra S., a Chilean woman, had the following experience (translated from Spanish to English) in 2000:

"It was week 34 of the pregnancy. I was

hospitalized for preeclampsia. On the third day, I began to feel sick. I hurt all over. Everyone was running around and they were going to do an urgent C-section. When they did the ultrasound, I began to see an intense and brilliant light. I said, "The light. The light!" The doctor said, "Open your eyes Alejandra."

Then, I went through this light. I had a feeling of extreme happiness, unmatched peace, and a feeling of universal love. I think I was in this state for about 45 minutes. I didn't see anyone in the light, but I experienced happiness as I had never felt before.

When I came back, my daughter had been delivered and they were suturing me with just a little anesthesia. During the "loss of consciousness," as the medics called it, I felt a lot of pain.

A year passed I was in charge of carrying out examination tests in a clinic. I had a patient with dementia, who never met my gaze with his. He brought his disabled daughter and we both talked for a long time.

They let me know when they would come
every month for the tests. I would be looking
for a taxi with a wheelchair.
The years passed, and I was promoted to the
boss of the laboratory. I received a phone call
and it was the daughter of my patient.
Between tears she told me that she would no
longer come with her father because he had
died. She was very sad. Due to her disability,
she hadn't been able to help him at the
moment when he had the attack. I tried to
comfort her, telling her about my NDE and
said to her that when her father died, he went
into the beautiful and fantastic light. He was
feeling no pain and that everything was
beautiful.
Then on hearing my story she started to cry
and she said to me that she had dreamed of
her father, and that he had said to her in her
dreams, "Talk to Alejandra who has
something to tell you." Now she was so sure
that this was what I had to tell her, so she
could have peace with the death of her father.
She said to me that she would go
immediately to visit the cemetery to tell him

that she had now talked to me and her anguish had been relieved."

Heidi C. went into labor on May 29, 2004. At the hospital, a nurse had to deliver the baby because the doctors were busy performing C-sections. A healthy baby boy was born. However, the placenta did not release as it should have. The doctor came and pulled the umbilical cord to get the placenta, but the cord tore off with the placenta still in her. She was admitted to surgery to remove the placenta.

As they rolled me into the operating room, my first thought was that it didn't look like what you see on TV. It was very small, sterile, and silver. The scene was surreal. As the anesthesiologist was placing the oxygen mask over my face and telling me to count backwards from 50. I thought to myself, "Do not go to sleep, stay awake." The next thing I know, I woke up in heaven or what I like to call "home". I had nobody but I was me. I was surrounded by angels, loved ones, Jesus, and God. We were all part of this radiant, warm and beautiful light. We were all connected and we were all one. The oneness was deeply profound and breathtaking.

They were there, loving and supporting me. The light was the most beautiful white, golden light.

I felt immense happiness, contentment, peace, warmth and love. The light was bubbly, sparkling and effervescent, like champagne.

There are no words to really express or articulate how I felt or to describe the beautiful light and warmth that I was bathed in. The colors and feelings were a million times magnified. The first feeling I had was that of being unconditionally loved. I say "feeling" because it was more than just a thought. I truly, deeply and profoundly felt the love through my entire being.

No words were spoken and everything was communicated by thought. My questions were answered before I could finish my thought. In fact, they were answered as I started thinking about the question. I kept feeling and receiving three messages over and over, again. I received these messages separately but at the same time. Time as we know it does not exist there, as it does here. The messages that I received were that I was unconditionally loved; that everything is always how it's supposed to be; and that everything would always be alright. I knew that if I didn't go back that my children, husband, family and friends would be okay. I wanted to stay but I was not given the option to stay.

I woke up with the doctor yelling at me to "wake up" and "open my eyes" The warmth and light were gone and I was cold, I was angry to be back in my body and back in the physical world. I was angry at the doctor for being so mean when he was waking me up and the fact that he woke me up, I wanted to go back "home."

The next morning in the recovery room, I told my husband what happened. I'll never forget the way he looked at me. It was a look of embarrassment and shame. He told me that I was crazy and that it had to have been a dream. In that moment, I decided not to tell anyone because if my husband didn't believe me, then who would? It would be 6 to 7 years before I finally told someone about my NDE.

I knew that something happened and I found out what it was ten years later when I ordered my medical records. My heart stopped in the operating room. The medical report stated that I had complications due to a heart disease called Mitral Valve Prolapse (MVP)....

I went into a depression and for the first couple of weeks after my NDE I wanted to go "home." I felt guilty and ashamed because I had three beautiful babies to take care of. To me my "real" home is in the spirit/soul world where there was no judgment, no suffering, no disapproval; just pure joy, creativity, peace and love.

I had been through so many challenging times leading up to my NDE and after years of feeling lost, alone and giving up hope, I no longer had faith. I had become disillusioned but after my NDE, I knew that even in my darkest hours when I felt isolated and separated that I was never alone. I knew that I was loved beyond measure. I had hope again.

My life changed drastically after my NDE. I started making positive changes in my life. I started to figure out who I was as a person, what I liked, what I wanted, and most importantly - that I needed to love myself. When I started to realize that I was ...

worthy and deserving of love, I started to change. For some of my friends and family it, was too much of a change. I lost some of my family and friends along the way.

Three years after my NDE, I filed for divorce after my husband cheated on me with my long-time best friend. I had finally had enough!...

On March 28,2011,1 received a call that my mom had a stroke. She passed away 2 days later

In September of 2014,1 received a letter from my landlord that my rent was going up $200 a month. I didn't know how I was going to pay the rent let alone the bills. I had used all

*of my savings and cashed out my retirement
to help supplement my income over the
years.*

*With the rent increase, I was in financial
distress.*

*That evening I fell to my knees, crying and
praying to God. In that moment of despair, I
clearly heard the 3 messages that I received
during my NDE and I knew, I just KNEW
that everything would be okay. The next
morning, I woke up and found an affordable
apartment. In March of 2015, I was hired on
permanently, which included a raise and
benefits.*

*I know that my experience was a gift and the
messages that I received continue to guide
me and help me get through this life. I do
believe that we are all one and that we are all
connected. Yes, I've had a life full of
obstacles but I have never been happier or
content with my life than I am right now. I
may not have it all, but I most definitely am
surrounded by wonderful, supportive and
loving family and friends, and that makes
what I don't have less important.*

I now have hope in the face of challenges, hardship and loss and I never lose sight of the light. I know that I'm never alone because I am unconditionally loved. I know that everything is always as it's supposed to be and even in my darkest moments I know that everything will be okay.

It might not be tonight, tomorrow or the next day, but it will be okay."

I know that giving back is extremely important, and I volunteer when I can. I have learned that you have to trust your intuition no matter what and listen to that voice; to trust that thought and do what you have to do. I have learned that your past does not define you. It was not a life sentence, but it was a life lesson – to paraphrase an ancient Buddhist proverb.

I have learned that you have to love yourself and that there is always something to be thankful for. Everything is ok in the end. If it's not okay, then it's not the end. And, most importantly, I have learned that joy is the experience of knowing that you are unconditionally loved and that nothing, not even death, can take that love away.

Here is one of my favorite quotes; it's from the marvelous blind writer Helen Keller: *"Keep your face to the sunshine and you cannot see the shadow. Its what sunflowers do."*

Dean B. was driving on Highway D1 on May 10, 2003, in Prague. Rain had made the road wet. This account was translated from Czech to English:

"The car started hydroplaning from the water on the highway. At 115km/per hour [71mph] the back of car kept bouncing to the right. I was in fifth gear, so I pushed hard on the clutch and the brakes in the same time. It didn't help much. I gripped the wheel firmly with both hands and then I looked up and screamed, because I was heading right toward the center barrier. I was screaming, pushing the pedals, turning the wheel and still it was coming closer, like a big wall that I couldn't escape.

I saw the first flash of light, two to three

meters before the center barrier—flashes as if somebody was taking pictures of me. Then came a recent memory, and then another flash of memory. It was going backwards in time towards the past.

I saw all these memories like when I had good times and felt lucky in love. Then I saw when I was back in kindergarten. I saw all my friends, family members, and scenes of nature. There were about fifteen to twenty flashes, and with one of the last flashes I saw somebody standing above me while I was in a stroller.

Then, I was in a tunnel. I was consumed by the darkness all around me. I felt like I was in a bathtub full of water with a sweet strawberry smell. It was a very nice feeling of total relief and release, like when you are about to get into a nice full bath.

Then, I saw a sharp, white light in the distance. It was very sharp but it didn't blind me and my eyes didn't hurt from it. In the center of the light there were myriad glittering rainbow colors. It was like the white xenon light on a mobile phone when

you are taking pictures. Suddenly,
I felt a strong push away from this white
light and all the beautiful feelings and
thoughts disappeared into nowhere. I was
very disappointed by this.
I opened my eyes and was sitting in the car
in the opposite direction on the highway.
Cars were passing by me. They were trying
to avoid the chain of cars crashing.
It was a strange feeling. I released myself
from the safety belt and got out of the car. I
was wet and probably in shock....
Later on nothing really happened to me,
except my hair got grayer. And when it
rains, I drive more safely and more slowly. If
anyone is interested, I tell them the story
and reassure that there is no need to be
afraid of death. I tell them that death is not
an end, only another dimension and with
only good qualities. A place where
experiences happen and time doesn't
matter."

Zdenka had a car accident in 2003 in
Slovenia, which brought on her NDE.
"By the laws of everyday physics, I shouldn't

be alive today. But I am alive, so I decided to share my experience by my best ability to comprehend what really happened.

It was about 6:30 in the morning, as I was driving on a highway to work. The rush-hour traffic was very busy, with cars speeding all around me, but I could still maintain our traveling speed of 120 km/h [75mph], which is lower than the allowed speed of 130 km/h. Then the rain started to pour down. Before I could reduce my speed, I drove into pooling rainwater that gathered on the road, a classic case of hydroplaning.

At that moment, I was surrounded by at least five cars on my right, and more cars behind me. My car got pulled from the water and I crashed into the highway fence on my left side.

The car got bounced and started to spin around over the road.

It all happened at once.

Instinctively, I stretched my arms and legs to fix myself into the seat. I was staring into the windshield; listening intently and waiting to crash into a car beside me. By logic of [the] situation, there had to be a crash. Let me here point out another fact. Outside it was pretty dark and because of the rain the visibility was like gloomy, wet twilight. So, with eyes wide opened, I was expecting the crash while spinning around and around.

The windshield turned milky, bright white. The inside of the car was absent of any sound, any movement or change. It was like I was spinning in [a] white room. I felt the spinning of the car, but nothing else was moving. It was like I would spin in one spot. As much as I felt, the car should have made at least three full spins around itself. But all I could see outside was this white surrounding the road, no other cars, nothing else. I can't say how long this lasted, maybe five seconds, ten seconds, or twenty seconds. I wouldn't know as there was no orientation on that, but it did seem like [a] prolonged time of spinning and staring in white and waiting for the impact.

Impact came, but much different than I expected. It was the sound of a crushing car when it landed. My body bounced. Instantly, the white was lifted, and the windshield turned dark again with rain falling on it. I was there again, on the road. The car did hit the fence and stayed glued to it. The car was turned around, facing back from where I came. "I'm alive!" was my first happy thought.

For a moment, I stared at the cars speeding directly towards me. "I must get out, before someone hits me just now!" I couldn't use the driver's door as I would step out directly in front of cars and the other door was blocked by the fence.

. . The electricity in car was still working. So I pulled down the side window, even grabbed my bag from the seat by moving over, and climbed out into the middle space between two highway fences. Just then the car died and front lights went out....

The pain in the neck arm and leg was all the pain I felt. It took 20 scary minutes before the police came and put out warning signs, but no one crushed into my car during that time. I'm still happy for that, too.

111

After this, I was in quite a shock for [a] few days, mostly because I was so happy. I was still alive. I just couldn't believe it! My friend said, "God has still plans with you, so angels saved you." Maybe, but it is unbelievable.

I was thinking about this a lot. About my reactions, how at that time my brain worked [in] high efficiency. I thought about how I climbed on back seats and opened a window there by hand. How I took a bag and phone in it. How I didn't panic until few hours later when I started to shake. What I saw and experienced is not so difficult to describe as it is difficult to understand....

My only explanation comes from science fiction, like moving to another dimension or another space-time. Can our reality be bended this way? If I moved, did I cause it myself or was it caused by some other force? Whatever it was, I was saved by some kind of miracle, unbelievable luck, or something. Surely, I'm grateful for every day that is given to me since then and sometimes I think that this time is somehow borrowed and not meant to actually be mine.

What do you think about all this? You've read accounts from both men and women; plus, these testimonies span decades and many countries. Let's summarize them and look for similarities:

Name	M/F	Saw Light?	Feelings	Fought Return?	Saw Diety?	New Peace?
Taylor	F	Colors	Euphoric	No	No	Yes
Keith	M/F	Brilliant	Warm & Loving	No	Jesus	Yes
Richard	M/F	Bright	Peaceful	No	No	Yes
James	M/F	Bright	None	No	Jesus	???
Missy	F	Ye	Peace & Beauty	Yes	Jesus	Yes
Patricia	F	No	None	No	No	No
Alejandra	F	Yes	Extreme Happiness	No	No	Yes
Heidi	F	Golden	Peace & Love	Yes	Jesus	Yes
Dean	M	Flashes	Total Relief	No	No	Yes
Zdenka	F	Bright	None	No	No	???

After reading these accounts, we can ask the question: Who said the reaper is grim? Did you find any grim accounts above? Have you had one of your own? If so, how does it affect your behavior since then? Like Zdenka, do you have a sense of being given a second chance or living on borrowed time?

Doug (who once played basketball for

Oregon State University) was invited to his high school alma mater in Elgin, Oregon, for an alumni All-Star basketball game. It was the former greats versus the current varsity team. One of the younger players jumped up as Doug was rebounding and accidently drove his head into Doug's nose. It broke his nose and caused extensive bleeding. Before anyone realized it, Doug was bleeding out and lost consciousness.

Doug stopped breathing and remembers walking down a long tunnel to a bright light, but before he could pass into the light, a woman stepped in front of Doug. She raised her hand and told Doug to go back. It wasn't his time.

Shortly after Doug's resuscitation (and subsequent recovery), he went to his dad's home. His dad invited him into the study, where his father told him his grandmother died five years before Doug was born. His dad brought out a photo album and showed Doug pictures of his grandmother. Doug told his dad that she was the woman who had stopped him and told him: "Go back. It's not your time."

Rajiv Parti, MD (1975-) is an anesthesiologist in southern California. Two years after his prostate cancer surgery, things were (literally) not going well. His body developed sepsis, and he was taken to UCLA Hospital on Christmas Eve 2010 for surgery. As he recounts, *"Fifteen minutes after general anesthesia was administered, I saw myself floating... ten feet above the operating table. My first reaction was: 'How is this possible?'"*

Next, he could "sense and see" his mother and sister in India. They were sitting at a table chatting about shopping. He even accurately described the clothes they were wearing that day. Afterwards, he saw himself being cut and could smell the infected mass as it was coming out of him. Then, he distinctly remembered the anesthesiologist tell a joke. (He later let the doctor know he heard the joke.) Following that, he was taken to a pitch-dark area where he describes a "thunderstorm, crying, and railing." Then he experienced painful torture. *"I realized I was a very mean person. Then, my father showed up and took me out of the hellish shell and led me towards a tunnel, where there was a bright light outside."* While traveling through the tunnel, he had a life review.

At the end of the tunnel, I was met by two robust young men. They were full of peace, but full of Strength. Telepathically, they told me they were my guardian angels. It was very surprising to me (a Hindu) that these two angels showed up.

My wife said: "What happened to the thousands of Hindu gods and goddesses? None of them showed up?"

"From there, I was guided to a meadow. The meadow was beautiful, with roses of different colors. A clear water stream was flowing, and there was a sweet smell to the air. As I

went higher and higher in the realm, my conscious became more formless, and then I found myself in front of a light. The light was like a thousand suns but was not hurting the eyes."

"I felt unconditional love. I could see love, I could hear love, I could taste love, and I could smell love. Love was all around. The best way he could describe it is a Sanskrit word, shanti, which is a prayer for cosmic peace, harmony, and bliss."

Parti continues: *"The Light Being talked to me— that my life would be spared, and when I go back it will be a totally different life. I would have to give up materialism, maybe my position as chief anesthesiologist, and be a healer of the soul."*

When he woke up "with a jolt," his first reaction was a desire to "go down on my knees and thank Heaven for the experience." Of course, he could not physically pull that off with all the things he was attached to. Parti was released seventy-two hours later. True to his vision, he decided to focus on "diseases of the soul," which he describes as depression, addiction, and chronic pain.

Laurin Bellg, MD (1964 -) is a pulmonologist (ICU) in Wisconsin. She recounts the interaction she had with a patient she performed surgery on. During the surgery, he had coded, that is, had a cardiopulmonary arrest. At a follow-up visit, *"two days later, he began telling me about me, and what he saw. He told me about my chartreuse and green shirt. He commented that the color glowed. He described to me events I knew to be true."*

Bellg recounts how the surgery team had a humorous moment during his code:

"I got kind of tangled in the bed with my stethoscope. As I was trying to pull it out of my pocket... pens came flying out."

The patient later commented:

'There was so much stuff in that pocket, I thought a frog was going to come out next."'

New findings presented at the Fifth European Academy of Neurology

Congress by researchers from the Rigshospitalet, Copenhagen University Hospital, University of Copenhagen in Denmark, the Center for Stroke Research in Berlin, and the Norwegian University of Technology in Norway.

Experiences most frequently reported by participants in the new study included:

Abnormal time perception (87 percent); Exceptional speed of thought (65 percent);

Exceptionally vivid senses (63 percent); and

Feeling separated from or out of their body (53 percent).

Those who experienced NDEs variously described feeling at total peace, having their "soul sucked out," hearing angels singing, being aware they were outside their body, seeing their life flashing before them and being in a dark tunnel before reaching a bright light. Others spoke of being aware of another's presence before they went to sleep, or of a demon sitting on their chest while they lay paralyzed unable to move.

"Over the years, I had experiences like this—where patients would come back and describe perfectly (outside of the physical) what happened in the physical. We knew they were experiencing cardiac death and could not possibly, by our definition, describe what they described."

In Atlanta, Georgia, a young woman named Pam was under the observation of cardiologist Michael Sabom, MD (1954-). She had a dangerous aneurism in her brain that required a very sophisticated surgery prep. Her body temperature was lowered to about 12°C, her heart and brain activity stopped, and the blood was drained from her head. Beyond, say, an induced coma, Pam would be clinically dead for approximately sixty minutes!

Her neurosurgeon was Robert Spetzler MD (1944 -) Pre-op prep included taping her eyes shut and placing probes (like foam ear plugs) in both her ears. Once she was fully anesthetized, Spetzler used the cranial saw to incise her skull. Pam said she remembered the top of her head tingling *"and I just [sort of] popped out of the top of my head. I was then looking down at my body... I knew it was my body."*

Pam's vantage point was as if she were perched on the surgeon's shoulder.

"I remember the instrument in his hand. It reminded me of an electric toothbrush."

She was told they would use a saw to open her skull, but what she beheld *"looked more like a drill than a saw. It even had little bits in a case."*

Next, she remembers hearing a female voice saying, "We have a problem; her arteries are too small." A male voice said, *"Try the other side."* It freaked Pam out that these voices were coming from the far lower side of the operating table because she thought, *"This is brain surgery."*

It turns out the cardiologist needed to access her femoral artery on the left or right of her groin. Indeed, it is a fact that the first try was not successful, so the other side was used.

After the successful surgery, Spetzler was told what Pam related to Sabom. His take: *"I don't think that the observations she made were based on what she experienced as she went into the operating room theatre ... for instance, the drill, and those things, were not visible. They were all covered up in their packages."* Spetzler describes the point in the surgery during the exchange between him and the cardiologist attempting to tap Pam's femoral artery for the heart/lung machine.

"At that stage of the operation, nobody can observe or hear in that state. I find it inconceivable that [by] normal senses, such as hearing [let alone the fact that she had clicking modules in each ear], that there was any way to hear those through normal auditory pathways."

Pam continues:

"I felt a Presence. I sorta turned around to look at it. That's when I saw a very tiny

pinpoint of light. And the light started to pull me,.. and I felt a physical sensation to the pulling." The closer she got to the light, she began to discern recognizable figures. "I distinctly heard my grandmother calling... and I went to her, and it felt great. I saw an uncle who passed away when he was only thirty-nine years old, and I saw many people I knew and many I didn't. I knew I was somehow connected to them."

"I asked if God was the light, and the answer was: 'No, God was not the light. The light is what happens when God breathes.' I distinctly remember thinking: 'I'm standing in the breath of God.' At some point in time, I was reminded that it was time to go back." She resisted her uncle, who was saying things like, "Honey, you've got to go," after he brought her back to "the body." Finally, she says he pushed her in! "I saw the body jump. I felt it."

Sabom summarizes:

"This is a classic near-death experience occurring under extremely monitored medical conditions where every known vital

sign, and clinical sign of life and death, was being monitored at the time; and that's what makes her case so remarkable and so valuable to us."

Finally, I want to share a story of my friend, R. C. "Bob" Giles. He is a pastor in Longview, Washington. He is not my pastor, as I don't attend church services. but he did officiate at my mother's funeral years ago.

Here is Pastor Giles's account:

"I was in the ICU at St, Johns Hospital, bleeding profusely from many areas. A nurse was by my side. When I felt like I was leaving, I said to her, "I think I'm leaving you right now." She said, "What are you doing?" I said, "I'm dying." She took my blood pressure and said, "You don't have anything!" She called some number, then people seemed to come from everywhere there and they started working on me.

Afterwards, I left my body and was up in the ceiling area; looking down. I was right next to the fluorescent light. That is, my spirit was. My body was still down below.

I could see all they were doing to me. I observed them put fifteen units of blood in my body before I was to go into surgery. I don't know how long it took them (I was not aware of time) to get fifteen units of blood in me. They put it in both arms and right in my neck. They put it in from three different directions because they were trying to get more [blood] in than was leaking out. I could see the nurse next to my body say, "Don't leave us! Don't leave us!"

I do remember that I was not in any pain as I was up there, but I don't remember going back into the body. I recently ran in to my surgeon from that day. Dr. Christine Katterhagen [1964-] said that mine was an inexplicably quick recovery. This was the second of three times that God miraculously rescued me from death.

Shortly after my experience, I performed a funeral for a 39-year old woman and shared my story during her service. Her doctor attended the memorial and told me afterwards - that he fully believed my account because a number of his patients had similar experiences."

Skeptical? Many people are. In 2012, Stuart Hameroff, MD, Professor Emeritus at the Departments of Anesthesiology and Psychology and the director of the Center of Consciousness Studies at the University of Arizona has done scientific research over the past few decades, utilizing the field of quantum mechanics in his pursuit of studying consciousness.

According a Huffington Post article, in a near-death experience, Hameroff explains:

"When the heart stops beating, the blood stops flowing, and the microtubules lose their quantum state, the quantum information in the microtubules isn't destroyed. It's distributed to the universe at large, and if the patient is revived, this quantum information can go back to the microtubules. In this event, the patient says they had a near-death experience, that is, they saw white light or a tunnel or floated out of their body. In the event that the

patient is not revived [and the patient dies],
'it's possible that the quantum information
can exist outside the body, perhaps
indefinitely, as a soul."

His 1996 theory of consciousness is called Orch-OR (orchestrated objective reduction). He derived it with British mathematician and physicist Sir Roger Penrose, Professor Emeritus at Oxford. He is the author of "The Road to Reality: A Complete Guide to the Laws of the Universe".

What are microtubules? They are part of the structure of our brain cells that act as non-linear computers. In essence, they affect, and interact with, other information sources (within or without our brain) via a kind of Wi-Fi manifestation of cosmic proportions.

-Chapter 10-
Suicide & The Near-Death Experience

Many people who commit suicide believe

that doing so will eliminate their pain,

but in reality they're only transferring the pain to others -

their family, friends and their entire community.

Anonymous Survivor

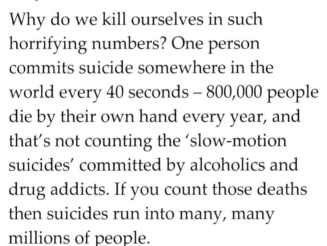

Why do we kill ourselves in such horrifying numbers? One person commits suicide somewhere in the world every 40 seconds – 800,000 people die by their own hand every year, and that's not counting the 'slow-motion suicides' committed by alcoholics and drug addicts. If you count those deaths then suicides run into many, many millions of people.

I can't begin to answer this terrible existential question, but because I've been studying "Near Death Experiences" for so many years I have a few thoughts to share with you. Most importantly, I believe that the stories told by suicides who have returned from near-death give us a special perspective on the meaning of our lives and the purpose of our existence on Earth.

Let's begin by noticing that many studies of NDE have concluded that people who commit suicide have a higher proportion of NDE than any other group – heart attacks, auto wrecks, being shot or stabbed, 'accidentally' overdosing, or experiencing any other uncontrolled as opposed to intentional cause of death. Some studies have concluded that as many as 25-30% of all suicide survivors report some form of NDE, and they are often profoundly emotional and spiritual experiences. I think that's a clue we should pay attention to very carefully.

The messages that these suicides receive from those they encounter on the other side also stand out from most other NDE experiences. A large majority of all kinds of non-suicide NDE messages are that your life isn't over and you can choose to go back if you wish. These NDE messages usually stress the voluntary aspect of the decision to return to life. Suicides are almost always met by spirits who gather around the new suicide with a special intensity, telling them that they must return, that their purpose in life has not been fulfilled, and that no matter how frightening, depressing or painful their life is, it must be lived to its natural end. Suicides are often virtually ordered to return and get their life together, to go back and stop hurting themselves and others, to repair the damage they have done, and then to go on and live their life as it was meant to be.

That message is well-illustrated by the story told by Karl, an Afghan War veteran:

"To this day I can't explain why I killed myself, but at the time it seemed like the only thing to do. Back from my second tour in Afghanistan, my wife and kids happy as hell that I was home for good, everybody

thanking me for my service – why was I so messed up that I felt like I had to get out of here no matter what? I was tired of the drinking and the drugs – my family life was a total wreck. I was just tired of the nightmares, the sweats, the chills, and the anger that soaked into every corner of my life like poison. I was so far gone that I even thought I was being considerate – no gun to the head and brains all over the place like too many guys I knew had done to their families. I figured a simple overdose on my pain meds and that would be it. Clean and tidy. I had plenty of pills. I waited until my wife and kids were gone to her Mom's "just for the weekend" and I just went into the garage, climbed into my car and did it.

I guess I figured that would be all she wrote, and sure enough I faded fast after I swallowed the pills with a beer chaser. Last thing I remember is thinking – "This isn't going to be so bad."

Then I felt myself moving through this tunnel at a very fast rate. I saw a light at the end of the tunnel and was wondering if this is where I was going. I didn't know if I was dead or alive at that point, but I do recall looking back at myself passed out on the front seat and I lay there completely oblivious to this other part of me which seemed to be heading towards something. "Is this what death is?" I wondered.

"No!" came an answer from somewhere. I was shocked to see a being of incredible beauty, radiating great love, great compassion and warmth. It was a being of beautiful, bright white light, which had silver threads emanating from the center. I was hesitant to say anything, and then I realized that my thoughts were being read by this incredible being of light. "No!" he repeated again. "This is not what death is like. Come, I will show you."

I remembered floating with him over to a pit of some sort that contained a very depressing landscape devoid of beauty and life, where people shuffled around with their heads down and their shoulders bent forward in total defeat. They wandered around aimlessly, bumping into each other and wailing. It was a horrifying thought that I was going to be cast down with these confused lost souls, but the voice seemed to understand my terror and relieved it with the following words: "This is a Hell of your own creation. After a very long time here you would have to go back to earth eventually and experience a new life all over again and you would be faced with the same difficulties that you faced in this lifetime. Suicide is not escape."

Then I was shown a panoramic view of my life. The years after my discharge which had become so burdened with alcohol abuse were the most painful part. I was shown a picture of the impact that alcohol had on my young children's life and the suffering that it would cause in their future. I saw the sorrow that my children would feel at the loss of their family and home because of me. I was shown that their mother would be destroyed and not take good care of them and eventually they would be put into a foster home. I saw that all three children, two boys and a girl, would follow my poor example and each would eventually use the bottle to escape life's day to day on-going stresses until each would then in turn become alcoholics also. The sight of my precious young daughter growing up, marrying a fellow alcoholic, who would eventually beat her and force incestuous relationships on their four daughters, was more than I could stand. I saw that if I returned to life and shaped up my act and began behaving like a responsible father and role model, all three children would grow up to be happy and productive. That doesn't mean completely free of the struggles of everyday life, but they would have a chance at making their own way, independent of any substance abuse. I saw how my oldest son was going to be able to become an important influential person in his time if I stayed around and behaved like a real father. I saw the downside of this future if I stayed in their relationship as the drunken weak father that he would eventually turn to drugs and end up in prison for crimes that he committed while trying to get money for drugs. It was

terrifying to me and I decided right then and there this was not what I wanted for my children, or myself. I was shown if I continued as a hopeless, pathetic drunk that I would not be able to escape. I would have to relive all the trials and traumas that brought me right up to the point of suicide this time, and that I would have to face those again in another life. It was more terrifying than I even wanted to admit. I cried uncontrollably. The being of light seemed to understand that I was filled with a sense of remorse, and then he showed me true compassion and love. He said in a stern voice but that was still like a father speaking to a son, "Your life is not yours to do with as you please. Did you create yourself? Did you give yourself life? No. Neither can you choose death." I couldn't speak, I couldn't think. My tears exhausted me. Then I realized – this presence must be Grace sent to me. The voice, now softer continued, "I'm not done with you, your work isn't finished, go back and do what you were meant to do."
Since my experience, I have found that I no

longer fear death, that I have a much more spiritual outlook and that I take my responsibility of raising my children very seriously now. I am there for them and I am proud to announce that their lives are coming along much better now that I have become the father I should have always been. I will never forget my experience on the edge of Hell and what it has taught me. I also realize that my negative Near-Death Experience was not negative at all when so much good has come out of it. I am now a pastoral counselor and do some bookkeeping for small businesses on the side. My children are on their own and have happy, busy, productive lives. I feel at peace."

A Vietnam Veteran told his support group of wanting to die after a terrible tragedy left him feeling hopeless and alone.

"He told of how years before he had been looking forward to the family reunion being held to celebrate his safe return from Vietnam and his new job. His entire family of nine people including his wife and

children had been riding in two cars following each other on the way to pick him up from work when a terrible fiery wreck with a gasoline tanker occurred on the freeway and all nine of his family were burned to death. He shared the shock and the numbness, the utter disbelief of surviving a year at war then coming home to start building a new life with a wife and children and extended family around him and then suddenly finding himself alone and childless, thrown into a life without a single close relative. He told of his total inability to come to grips with any of it.

He then shared how he changed almost overnight from a husband and father to a total bum, drunk every day from morning to night, using every conceivable drug and trying to commit suicide in every conceivable way, yet never able to succeed. His last recollection was that after two years of literally bumming around, he found himself lying on a dirt road at the edge of a forest, drunk and stoned as he called it, trying desperately to be reunited with his family. Not wanting to live, not even having the energy or will to move out of the road even when he saw a big truck coming toward him and then running over him.

Then he saw himself in the road broken and bleeding, dying, but observing the whole scene of the accident from a few feet above. Then he told how with no transition his family appeared in front of him, in a glow of light with an incredible sense of love. They had happy smiles on their faces, and simply made him aware of their presence, not communicating in any verbal way but in some form of thought transference, letting him know the joy and happiness of their present existence. He was not able to tell us how long this reunion lasted. He was so awed by his family's health, their beauty, their radiance and their total acceptance of this present situation, by their unconditional love. He tells how at their urging he made a vow not to come toward them or embrace or to try to follow them, not to try to join them now but only later, but to re-enter his physical body now so that he could share with the world what the wonder of what he had experienced. This, he remembers thinking, would be redemption for his years of trying to throw his physical life away in every way possible.

Immediately after making this vow , he was back above the road watching the truck driver carry his broken body to the side of the road. He saw an ambulance speeding to the scene of the accident. Then in a flash he saw himself being taken into the emergency room and people leaning over him and then, at that moment, he recalls re-entering his physical body. He tells of getting off the ER bed, in spite of attempts to stop him, and starting to move around. Although he had multiple broken bones and huge lacerations on his upper body his legs were OK and he remembers being able to move without pain and speak to the doctors and nurses clearly. At that moment he told them of making a commitment that he would not die until he had the opportunity of sharing the existence of life after death with as many people as would be willing to listen.

Throughout his recovery from being nearly crushed to death and his months of physical rehab at the VA, he never had delirium tremens or any aftereffects from his years of heavy constant abuse of drugs and alcohol. He felt healed and whole inside and his body healed remarkably quickly. The doctors and therapists said they couldn't explain the speed of his complete recovery."

What NDE Tells Us About Ending Pain Through Suicide

Many people who commit suicide believe that doing so will eliminate their pain, but in reality they're only transferring the pain to others - their family, friends and their entire community. Their family is left to grieve and wonder if they are somehow to blame. Children of suicides are at much higher risk of suicide themselves and almost always say that it's because they feel guilty and ashamed. Spouses often want nothing more than to join their loved one in death, even though before the suicide their lives may have been stable, productive and even happy and even after their loss they may objectively have much to live for. Furthermore, everything we know about suicide and NDE shows us that the pain and suffering that lead to suicide stay with the person after death. Nobody wins – everybody loses. That's why the messages we have from suicides who have NDEs and come back to tell their story have so much enlightenment to share with those still alive who may also be thinking of ending their life.

"Recovering from the suicide of a loved one, you need all the help you can get, so I very much recommend a meditation program. The whole picture of how to recover from this has to do with body, mind, and spirit. That's applicable to any kind of depression."
Judy Collins

Elsewhere in this book we've discussed the beliefs of various religions regarding suicide and noted that for the most part they condemn suicide as a violation of God's intent for mankind. There are certain religions, or really just branches of certain religions, that profess that the dying for a holy cause will get you a better place in the afterlife. Of course, once you commit suicide by blowing yourself up there's no body left to come back to – so there are no Jihadis telling us of their NDE and being met by however many virgins they thought were waiting for them in Paradise. With a suicide bomber, dead men really do tell no tales – they can't because they are in little pieces. But it's also instructive to note that somehow it is always the leaders in these bizarre religious sects who tell their followers to go commit "holy suicide" while they live on, usually in some comfort and even luxury.

"Some people are willing to be killed for beliefs for which the people from whom they got them are not even willing to be slapped."
Mokokoma Mokhonoan

Depression And Suicide

Depression comes from many different forms, and I believe that most people who want to or do commit suicide could be saved if they had the proper treatment for the underlying depression that is haunting them. Certainly not all, but many people who commit suicide have major depression that is associated with some terrible event or set of conditions that have made life seem not worth living. Winston Churchill called depression a "Black Dog" that attacked him often and without warning.

What can a person facing depression do, other than simply taking meds and hoping for the best? You can start or go to a depression support group meeting and ask for help. Finding a depression support group may be easy or difficult depending on where you live though there are online options for some of the groups so even if you are in an area where a group does not meet, you can still be a part of a support group. You can search online to find a nearby group simply by googling "Depression Anonymous near me". Once you've located a support group that is close by, reaching out to join may be scary, but once you attend your first meeting I can promise from personal experience that it will get easier. It will also help if you can tell your family your real thoughts and of course you should consider getting professional help, but the real healing will begin when you decide to get over yourself and go help others - nothing is better for coming out the other side of depression than getting out of your own head to help someone else rather than lamenting how nobody is helping you. When you join a support group you'll hear many people tell the same story – how their lives began to heal the moment they decided to begin helping others. After all isn't loving and being kind to others and receiving their goodness and love in return what most of us really wanted to do with our life originally? Re-affirming this attitude can be a giant first step toward recovery from depression.

"The suicide arrives at the conclusion that what he is seeking does not exist; the seeker concludes that what he has not yet looked in the right place."

Paul Watzlawick

A well-known spiritual healer described this way the messages they receive from suicides who for whatever reason have not been able to return to life and must deal with the consequences of the finality of their act.

"It's very important that those coming through acknowledge what they've done. It's like getting up at an AA meeting and saying, 'I'm an alcoholic.' Coming forward and saying, 'I have taken my own life' is part of many suicide NDEs.

A friend of mine who had recently taken his life came through and did not know how to go into the light I kept telling him to go forward to the light, but he was afraid of judgment. He couldn't forgive himself. Also, he was having a problem with the fact that after he had taken his own life, his spirit obviously lingered around the scene of the act. He could not overcome the memory of his father's discovering him, and that was haunting him emotionally to a tremendous degree in the next dimension. What he and many of us don't understand is that there is judgment there, but it is not done by a majestic being on a throne. Judgment rests basically with yourself. And we all know that the greatest enemy we can face is ourselves.

It can take eons of time as we understand it before they can go forward into the light. It depends on the person. You're in control, even after life on Earth has ended. You hold the reins. Those who've come through those darker levels have said that they've had to face themselves and realize that if they don't shape up, in other words, learn more about themselves, they're not getting anywhere."

Attitude Matters

"The longer I live, the more I realize how much impact attitude has on people's lives. A person's attitude is more important than any amount of education. It's more important than money, circumstances, failures, successes, appearance or skill. It's especially more important than what others think, say or do. Attitudes are what make or break a person, a family, a company, a church, a community – or an entire country. The remarkable thing is that a conscious change in attitude is something we can each make happen every day of our life. Every day we have choices we can make regarding the attitude we embrace. Sometimes those choices are very difficult, and there's no shame in asking for help. Nobody has all the answers, as I've said elsewhere. We cannot change the past, nor the fact that other people will act a certain way. We cannot change the inevitable – gravity will always operate regardless of our attitude toward it. But we can change our attitude in ways that will affect 90% of what happens around us

and to us. And we're the only ones who can change our real, true attitude – not just the face we show to the world.

I am convinced that life is 10 percent what happens to us and 90 percent how we react to it. So if we work to change how we think about and react to all crazy and often negative things that happen every day in this world, we might just find that we can change those aspects of the world itself – at least the world that we and our friend and family live in together. No hate toward ourselves or others; no violence toward ourselves or others; and no death of the Spirit."

(From "Attitudes", by Patrick Lockhart; NoHateNoViolence.com)

—Chapter 11—
Notable Quotables

"We hear tears loudly on this side of heaven. What we don't take time to contemplate are the even louder cheers on the other side of Death's valley."

Zig Ziglar 1926 - 2012

I ENJOY QUOTES from famous and successful people because they can be so inspiring! Whether it's Winston Churchill telling war-torn Britons "Never give in, never give in, never, never, never, never," or FDR telling anxious Americans, "The only thing to fear is fear itself," quotes live well beyond the men and women who speak them.

If you have, somehow, missed being inspired by the preceding pages, do not lose out on the following hope- filled, insightful, and even humorous quotes about death. I am amused, uplifted, and encouraged every time I read them.

"While I thought that I was learning how to live, I have been learning how to die."
Leonardo daVinci (1452-1519)
"Death has its revelations: the great sorrows which open the heart open the mind as well; light comes to us with our grief. As for me, I have faith; I believe in a future life. How could I do otherwise?"
Victor Hugo (1802-1885)
"Death is a challenge. It tells us not to waste time. It tells us to tell each other, right now, that we love each other."
Leo Buscaglia (1924 -1998)
"It seems to me that that if you or I must choose between two courses of thought or action, we should remember our dying and try so to live that our death brings no pleasure on the world."
John Steinbeck (1902-1968)
"We sometimes congratulate ourselves at the moment of waking from a troubled dream; it may be so the moment after death."
Nathaniel Hawthorne (1804-1864)
"Death gives meaning to our lives. It gives

importance and value to time. Time would become meaningless if there were too much of it."

Ray Kurzweil (1948-)

"Men fear death as children fear to go in the dark; and as that natural fear in children is increased by tales, so is the other."

Sir Francis Bacon (1561-1626)

"I know, beyond a shadow of a doubt that there is no death the way we understood it. The body dies, but not the soul."

Elisabeth Kubler-Ross (1926-2004)

"I thank my God for graciously granting me the opportunity of learning that death is the key which unlocks the door to our true happiness."

Wolfgang Mozart (1756-1791)

"Death and love are the two wings that bear the good man to heaven."

Michelangelo (1475-1564)

"Personally, I would be delighted if there were a life after death ... if it gave me a chance to discover how history turns out."

Carl Sagan (1934-1996)

"I'm not afraid to die, I just don't want to be

there when it happens.
Woody Allen (1935-)
"The goal of all life is death."
Sigmund Freud (1856-1939)
"How strange this fear of death is!
We are never frightened at a sunset."
George MacDonald (1824-1905)
"There is no death, only a change of worlds."
Chief Seattle (1786-1866)
"No one knows whether death, which men in
their fear apprehend to be the greatest evil,
may not be the greatest good."
- Plato (c. 428-347 BC)
"All that lives must die, passing through
nature to eternity."
Shakespeare (1564-1616)
"I intend to live forever, or die trying.
Groucho Marx (1890-1977)
"The only thing different, between death and
taxes, is that death doesn't get any worse
when Congress is in session."
Will Rogers (1879-1935)
"I have lived with the prospect of an early
death for the last 49 years. I'm not afraid of
death, but I'm in no hurry to die. I have so

much I want to do first."
Stephen Hawking (1942-2018)

—Chapter 12—
What Goes Around, Comes Around

"I'm not afraid of dying.
Total peace after death,
becoming someone else.
That's the best hope I've got."
Kurt Cobain 1967 - 1994

The concept of reincarnation is not a Western thought. It dates back thousands of years to the Hindus. Some people believe in reincarnation, that we die and return to live another life as a different person, animal, or insect. Some people, through hypnosis, go back to the unconscious mind, which may tell us about life at an earlier time.

One account I heard was about a man who was hanged from a tree for cattle rustling in the 1800s. He returned to human life in the 1930s and lived a normal life

Our unconscious mind holds many stories. One of my favorites is a lady

154

who, in an earlier life in Sweden, was married and had twelve kids. She lived into her eighties, then died, and came back in the 1940s to another life. She had unconscious recall of the earlier life in Sweden.

"A Dog's Purpose" by W. Bruce Cameron is a great read. It dramatically presents what the reincarnation of dogs could look like. If you have a chance to read the book, or see the movie, do it! It is a great story about living more than one life.

Non-religious evidence for the existence of reincarnation comes from two camps:

Past-life regression therapy of adults

First-person accounts of the past lives of complete strangers, as told by children

In his best-selling book *"Only Love Is Real"* (1997), Brian Weiss, MD (1944-) posits that we have one supreme being. Rather than revealing the identity of this supreme being, he suggests we call him, her, or it by whatever name fits our belief system (religion) of choice or ancestry. If you're a Muslim, you call this supreme being Allah; if you are a Jew, you call the supreme being YHWH; and so on. According to Weiss, you go before the Master at death to decide whether you go back to Earth to learn something you didn't learn in the first life. Weiss contends we may live several lives.

Weiss does not seem to fit the mold of a crackpot or quack. He has an undergraduate degree from Columbia University and graduated from Yale Medical Center in 1970. His internship led him to New York University Medical Center, from which he returned to Yale for a two-year residency in psychiatry. His career path eventually led to his becoming the head of psychiatry at Mt. Sinai Medical Center in Miami, Florida. The method he used to plumb the depths of one's psyche and deepest memories was hypnotism, a process that ushers one from the present to the ethereal.

In 1980, "Catherine," one of Weiss's patients, was suffering from recurring nightmares and anxiety attacks. She began talking about past life experiences under hypnosis. Astonishingly, she relayed messages that contained "remarkable revelations" of Weiss's family and even his deceased son. Weiss, like most of us in the West, did not believe in reincarnation at the time. Yet, when he later confirmed elements of Catherine's conversation, not only was his mind open to "the survival of an element of human personality after death," but he also became convinced of it. Weiss employed past-life therapy to cure Catherine of her torments.

Ian Stevenson (1918-2004) was a medical doctor and researcher. Stevenson is known worldwide for his research conducted over more than forty years on cases of de facto reincarnation and other evidence of survival after death. He was educated at St. Andrew s University in Scotland and McGill University in

Montreal, and he received his medical degree from McGill in 1943.

After a brief period of research in biochemistry, Stevenson looked for a way to study "something closer to the whole human being." In the late 1940s, therefore, he joined a group at New York Hospital and began research in psychosomatic medicine, particularly on the effects of stress and strong emotions on physical symptoms. This work eventually led him to training in psychiatry and psychoanalysis, and in 1957, he was appointed professor and chairman of the Department of Psychiatry at the University of Virginia. The discovery of numerous scattered reports of young children who seemed to have memories of a previous life led to the research that he pioneered for forty years. In T961, Stevenson made trips to India and Sri Lanka to conduct first-hand interviews of young children who had memories of a previous life. Stevenson was able to establish the

Division of Personality (now Perceptual) Studies at the University of Virginia, the only university-based research unit in the world devoted to the study of previous life memories, near-death experiences, and related phenomena. His empirical approach made him deeply skeptical of purported accounts of previous lives obtained by hypnosis or past life regression. He kept a file in his office, which he labeled "Extravagant Claims," containing numerous Thomas Jeffersons, Mary Magdalenes, Napoleons, and other famous people. The file was his smoking gun that hypnosis accounts were unreliable because, for instance, three people cannot have all been Napoleon Bonaparte in a past life.

Stevenson was the author of over three hundred publications, including fourteen books. In his publications on cases of the reincarnation type, he identified numerous recurring and cross- cultural patterns. These included the ages when children would typically speak about their memories (beginning at about two to three years and ending by seven or eight), the mode of death of the previous personality (often violent or sudden), unusual behaviors (including phobias, unusual skills or interests), and gender confusion (when the previous life was that of the opposite sex). His magnum opus was a two-volume, 2,268-page monograph reporting over two hundred cases in which highly unusual birthmarks or birth defects of the child corresponded with marks, usually fatal wounds, on the previous person.

In 1982, Stevenson was instrumental in the founding of the Society for Scientific Exploration, an organization for scientists involved in areas of research challenging many assumptions of contemporary science. The research and investigations were the embodiment of the Virginia University's founder, Thomas Jefferson: *"For here we are not afraid to follow truth wherever it may lead, nor to tolerate any error so long as reason is left free to combat it."*

After years of traveling to India, Sri Lanka, Alaska, Burma, and Thailand, Stevenson copiously compiled accounts of children with reported past-life memories. In addition to the common ages of remembering and then fading of memories for these children was that the culture they lived in believed in reincarnation.

A skeptic would discount the veracity of these memories/thoughts because of the pro-reincarnation environment (even among the Tlingit peoples in Alaska). Thus, we look at the seventy-nine cases Stevenson investigated in America—as reported in volume 171, number 12 of The Journal of Nervous and Mental Disease (1983). The abstract notes:

"Few American children make verifiable statements, and those who do nearly always speak about the lives of deceased members of their own families." When the doctor

161

believes the child's account(s) to be accurate, he refers to the "deceased member" as the child's "previous personality."

The abstract continues: *"Although many of the American cases may derive from fantasies, a wish-fulfilling motive or obvious gain for the child is not discernible in most of them."*

By his own statistics, at least 80 percent of the Asian children's accounts of past life experiences were verifiable (by Stevenson's standards). Conversely, only 20 percent of the American children's accounts were verifiable. Before we say "Aha," we must remember that Asian reports were timely and American reports were quite dated. The cause of so much time passing before the child's recollections are revealed had to do with the American parents not wanting their child to be stigmatized or considered abnormal. That is why the article appeared in a trade publication for child psychologists and pediatricians. After reading the article, they are armed with more data to share with the parents. Thus, as with any investigative trail, the more time has passed, the colder the trail gets.

Still, there were some similarities with the Asian children that were probative:

Children's Fears/Phobias.

These were ostensibly caused by the dears or phobias experienced by the prior personality or the manner of death experienced by the deceased. For instance, a child whose prior personality had died by drowning exhibited an irrational fear of bodies of water.

Children's Markings.

These coincided with damage to the previous personality's body (gunshot, stab wound, burn, etc.); Thus, a child with an unusual birthmark on the chest described a person who died of a stab wound to the chest in the same spot.

Gender Confusion.

A boy might have a prior personality that was a female. Inexplicably, the boy seems drawn to girl's clothing. Note some pro- reincarnation religions do not subscribe to cross-gender reincarnations. In some instances (Particularly in Asian NDE experiences), the child can speak a language or dialect without having been taught the language. It is considered a psychic phenomenon because it is unexplainable in scientific terms and is not replicable. When the child's previous personality is from a foreign people group and he or she speaks their language, it lends credibility to the child's memories.

Unexplainable Food Preferences.
It is believed the child can take on the food preferences of the previous personality. Often, such food hadn't been served in the household, yet the child yearns for a unique spice or food recipe.

DéjàVu Experiences.
Also known as veridical perception, this

is where a child acquires verifiable information that was unattainable by natural means.

Many of the children could accurately describe geographic features of another place they had never been to. When taken there, they exhibited a familiarity of surroundings that would only be accorded to locals. The children have that "hey. I've been here before" experience.

What makes these accounts fascinating is that parents can't possibly fake their child's birthmark or other birth defect. Nor would they be likely to coax them to cross-dress or to exhibit phobic behaviors towards weapons or bodies of water or eat foods they don't care for. That is, there is reliability to these accounts on the source side and an "easier read" on the interpretation side. So, what do you think? Has your child been there, done that? If so, the academics at the University of Virginia School of Medicine, Division of

Perceptual Studies would like to talk to you. They can be reached at DOPS@virginia.edu.

—Chapter 13—
Will I See My Loved One Again?

"Death is not extinguishing
the light; it is only putting
out the lamp because
the dawn has come."

Rabindranath Tagore 1861 - 1941

WE OFTEN HEAR that when we die we will be reunited with people and pets that have died before us. Whether it is a child, spouse, parent, grandparent, or any loved one who died, we suffer a crushing blow when we are left on Earth without the one we long to spend time with again.

What we know is that we are here in a fixed, physical place called Earth. What we may not know is where the deceased loved one is. Some may suggest Heaven. Some may suggest Hell. Some will say a distant star. Others will tell you they are probably on Earth somewhere, starting over as another person or life form.

This is why what we believe in is so important—because a strong belief system forms the core understanding of what that faith says will happen after one's last breath and heartbeat. It answers the questions: Is there a place of punishment? Is there a place of reward? Is there a safe place to go before an eternal judgment is made? Are we recycled? (Consider referring back to the chart of ten major beliefs or religions in Chapter 4.)

Now comes the hard part. If your faith prescribes a place of judgment or torment and it is likely that the loved one you lost is there, would you still want to be reunited? Could there ever be any fun or happiness in such a place? (By any reasonable measure, you'd have to say no.) Thinking beyond your wants, would that person want you to have to endure that too? Would he or she feel profoundly disappointed to see you there? Would it add to your loved one's punishment to conclude your punishment was (in some way) his or her fault?

Let's put the shoe on the other foot. You are the one who has been estranged from faith, but your loved one was all-in. He or she prayed, read the holy writings, sang the songs of the faithful, and even donated to its causes. Now this person is gone. Presumably, your loved one is where his or her hope for eternity resided and faith has become sight. How are you going to get there? What will it take? What must you not fail to do to see this person again?

As you answer these questions, you find there come not only a test of your faith but also a test of your will. One is useless without the other. It's like having zeal without knowledge.

An arrow cannot hit its mark effectively without two things: the point of the arrow that penetrates the target and the vanes (or fletching) of the arrow that deftly guides it to its destination. Your faith is your guide; my faith (or lack thereof) cannot be your guide. Your will is what makes your faith stick and causes you to live it out, no matter what the circumstances. Both your faith and your will can serve as an example to others. Just know that a lack of faith (or a lack of will) is also evident to those around you.

I would encourage you to be fully committed to the course you are bound to take. Have both feet in. That means setting goals and investing your time and energy to achieving them. I can't tell you how to be a good Buddhist, a good Jew, a good agnostic, or even a good Christian. These are things you discover for yourself. As you discover and connect, you will own your path, and it will become more real to you.

I do wish you the best journey to your desired destination ... with the happiest of reunions or revelations.

—Chapter 14—
Only the Good Die Young

"Some people die at 25
and aren't buried until 75."

Benjamin Franklin
1706 - 1790

"Abraham, Martin, and John," was a popular 1968 folk song by Dion and written by Dick Holler. It was a tribute to four assassinated Americans who had championed civil rights: Abraham Lincoln, Martin Luther King Jr., John F. Kennedy, and Robert "Bobby" Kennedy. At the end of each verse highlighting these men. Holler soliloquizes that "the good die young."

An amazing number of people we remember for the good things they did in their lives died way too young: https://www.deadoraliveinfo.com/diedyoung

Nine years later, Billy Joel recorded the hit song "Only the Good Die Young."

171

These two songs have influenced three generations, like it or not. But is it stating a fact or simply praising those who died young? What deaths were Americans lamenting that fueled this sentiment in the 1960s and beyond?

Do only the good die young? No... it just feels that way sometimes because it hurts to see a person (famous or not) die in his or her prime. Yet we see how many famous people lived to be one hundred!

Many famous people have made the much-admired and very exclusive "Century   Club" https://www.deadoraliveinfo.com/live dto100

One can't appreciate actor and comedian George Burns (1896-1996) becoming a centenarian until you know he chain-smoked fifteen to twenty cigars a day! On a Tonight Show interview, Johnny Carson (1925- 2005) asked Burns (then ninety^-three) what his doctor said about his smoking. Burns stared back at

Johnny and said matter-of-factly, *"My doctor is dead."* Johnny broke out in laughter (https://tinyurl.com/yexkocmh). English anthropologist Ashley Montagu (1905- 1999) summed it up this way: *"The idea is to die young as late as possible."* So what did Benjamin Franklin mean in his quote at the beginning of this chapter? That even twenty- five-year-olds can get into a monotonous routine of life and stay that way till they're put to rest at seventy-five. The implicit challenge is to live life fully every day and all day.

That is part of the beauty of thinking about your death. Yes, you will die, but you are alive now. You have capacities, thoughts, dreams, and talents now that others don't. So what are you going to do?

The mission of this book is to encourage foresight living and for you to approach the sunset of your life with high anticipation and low dread.

—Chapter 15—
Who Decides My Fate?

"I am the master of my fate.

I am the captain of my soul."

William Ernest Henley

1849 - 1903

JUDGING FROM Henley's poem, he appears to be an agnostic. In the first stanza, he writes: *"I thank whatever gods may be for my unconquerable soul."* We can disagree with what others believe, but the main thing is to be clear on what you believe. The Roman Paul of Tarsus (c. 4BC-c. 63 AD) said, *"Let every man be fully persuaded in his own mind."* That is why your answers to these questions need to come from you... not me. I am not the captain of your soul. It would be arrogant to pretend otherwise.

However, I must warn you to be very careful as to whom you do believe is the master of your fate. You need to place your security in things that are real, even if things appear

174

otherwise. We can be quite sure that many passengers on the RMS Titanic were very secure in boarding that (unsinkable) ship. It was, as we know, a fatal mistake.

Your ship must be built on your own faith and reason, but it also needs to square with natural and spiritual laws. If you hold your car keys five inches over a table and let go, natural/physical law will be evident as your keys fall to the tabletop. Try it again? Same result. Now, try saying, "I believe these keys won't fall next time," and do it again. Results? They fall again. They must obey the physical law of gravity. Gravity is a compelling force to be reckoned with. So much so that people fall for it. (Sorry, I couldn't help that.) I recognize there is a different kind of gravity to facing an eternal future. It is serious, but it doesn't have to be scary.

What are spiritual laws? They are comprised the things that are immutable in the spirit world. I do not approach this topic as an expert but, rather, as an observer. As best I can tell, the spiritual laws look like this:

Law of Dominion.

The spirit of a human is designed to dominate our minds. The spirit man or woman has inert capacity to affect our thoughts, our feelings, our actions, and our words. Spiritual people are exhorted to take every thought captive. Like playing Capture the Flag, your positive (or godly) spirit is to contend with negative (or evil) forces that foment negative thoughts and to rescue them off the roads of insecurity, depression, judgementalism, arrogance, and any other negative, life-draining force.

We can find many examples of people whose spirits overwrote their minds, specifically, the will to survive. Many US Medals of Honor were awarded to soldiers in WWII. One such soldier was a Marine from Mississippi named Jack Lucas (1928-2008). Barely seventeen years old, Lucas was with his unit fighting at Iwo Jima when two grenades rolled into the trench he and three other Marines occupied. Lucas yelled at the others to get out. One of the grenades went off and caused life-threatening injuries to Lucas. His body took on over 250 pieces of shrapnel, including six in his brain and two in his heart.

His Medal of Honor citation reads, in part:

"By his inspiring action and valiant spirit of self- sacrifice, he not only protected his comrades from certain injury or possible death, but also enabled them to rout the Japanese patrol and continue the advance."

Jack Lucas had the same human survival instincts that you and I have. So why didn't the flight mechanism of his mind cause him to flee the scene too?

Because his spirit overrode his mind and emotions. Even the president and Marine Corps acknowledged such by attributing his action to his "valiant spirit of self-sacrifice".

Law of Supernatural Powers.
Spiritual powers supersede natural forces. Because the spiritual universe (which we can't see) preceded the physical universe (which we can see), the former is not limited to the physical laws of the latter.

You may have heard about the account of the Hebrew military leader named Joshua (who came after Moses). His army was routing the Hebrews' opponents, but the day was far spent, and there wasn't enough time to finish the task. Thus, Joshua called upon the God of Abraham, Isaac, and Jacob to make the "sun and moon" stand still so the victory would be fulfilled. Other non-Hebrew cultures report a long day in that region; plus ancient peoples (the Maoris in New Zealand and the Culhuacans in Mexico) report a long night, as they were at the opposite side of the globe. That would be a clear example of the spiritual world overriding the physical world.

Harkening back to WWII, an army medic was among the troops trying to take a Japanese-fortified territory in Okinawa, called the Maeda Escarpment (AKA Hacksaw Ridge). There was a series of daily battles that resulted in the army retreating down a four-hundred-foot cliff each day. Private Desmond T. Doss (1919-2006) was the only soldier that did not carry a weapon of any kind. He was a medic who was a conscientious objector.

After one particular onslaught of relentless opposing forces, Doss (a man of unwavering faith) chose not to descend the cliff but stay in the midst of the occupied kill zone to rescue any comrades still living. By the end of that fateful night, he had single-handedly rescued seventy-five men! Keep in mind Doss had a very slight build, yet he dragged (or fireman-carried) men up to twice his size.

Not only that, but after all that taxing effort to get the wounded to the cliff's edge, he commanded his weary and taunt muscles to safely lower the men down four hundred feet by rope! However, the super-human actions of Desmond Doss didn't stop there. His 1945 Medal of Honor citation tells of an ensuing assault:

"On 21 May, in a night attack on high ground near Shuri [Okinawa], he remained in exposed territory while the rest of the company took cover, fearlessly risking the chance that he would be mistaken for an infiltrating Japanese and giving aid to the injured until he was himself seriously wounded in the legs by the explosion of a grenade.

Rather than call another aid man for cover, he cared for his own injuries and waited five hours before litter bearers reached him and started carrying him to cover. The trio was caught in an enemy tank attack and Private First Class Doss, seeing a more critically wounded man nearby, crawled off the litter and directed the bearers to give their first attention to the other man. Awaiting the litter bearers' return, he was again struck, this time suffering a compound fracture of one arm. With magnificent fortitude he bound a rifle stock to his shattered arm as a splint and then crawled 300 yards over tough terrain to the aid station."

You cannot persuade me that all this hero accomplished was pure adrenalin. Obviously, there was a spiritual force equipping this man (mentally and physically) to achieve the impossible. That is because spiritual powers eclipse natural limitations and physical laws.

Law of Conflict.

There is a war going on between good and evil spirits. We humans are in the crossfire. Indeed, we seem to be the territory being fought over in the spirit realm.

Because we are spirits, temporarily housed in a physical body, we serve (whether conscious of this fact) one or the other kings of the opposing spiritual forces. I know this is a big thing to swallow, but that doesn't discount the

181

truth of the matter. It is a great benefit to know which spiritual army you are serving.

Psychiatrists and theologians have extensive explanations of these opposing spiritual forces. You can personalize them as you wish.

Creator	Betrayer
Pure	Corrupt
Good	Evil
Righteous	Conniving
Father of Truth	Father Of Lies
Has Authority	Wants Authority
Willing To Sacrifice	Sacrifices Only Others
Operates By Conviction	Operates By Convincing
Says "I Am God"	Says "You Are God"
Gives Us Free Will	Takes Away Free Will
Uses Truthful Prophets	Uses False Prophets
Abides In Heaven	Abides In Hell
Wins In the End Of Time	Loses In the End Of Time

We have looked at some spiritual laws, and we have attempted to define the entities on each side of the spiritual divide. As we look at both sides, we can take stock of which king we tend to obey from day to day. If our introspection puts us squarely in an undesirable army, can we defect? I suspect we can, but I can't tell you how - other than suggest denying your citizenship in the kingdom you are in and pledging allegiance to the new king.

Recently, Meghan Markle married Prince Harry of England. As his bride, she had to become a citizen of England and pledge allegiance to the Queen. Going into it, she was born and raised a US citizen. Markle did not renounce her US citizenship and does not need to, but it remains to be seen if she will live with a dual-citizenship status. Though that is allowed in this physical realm, dual citizenship does not exist in the spirit realm. We belong to one or the other. Ignorance of the spirit world is no defense of its effect on your life on Earth, or wherever your spirit goes.

If you get nothing else out of this book, let it convince you that your essence is 100 percent spirit, which has a temporary body and a conforming soul. Which of these fixations best describes you?

The prideful are fixated on their body. The thoughtful are fixated on their soul. The enlightened are fixated on their spirit.

Being enlightened doesn't make you perfect, but it does give you a new perspective that more holistically results in a successful and meaningful life—and who doesn't want that?

Retired Army Cpl. Bill Vandenbush understands the need to share the experience. He was on patrol in Vietnam in April 1969 when U.S. forces dropped a bomb too close to his unit's position. The blast shredded his right side and destroyed his face. *"I thought I was going to die, so I took off my pac,"* Vandenbush said. *"Next thing I know, I'm in this dark corridor and I came out in this incredibly beautiful white light, so full of peace and this incredible energy. I had no concern about my life, no worries."*

He spoke with two "light beings" while he was in this euphoric state — one of them his grandfather, who promised to show him around. The other, however, told him he needed to go back. And return through the tunnel he did. *"I was told I would have a long and productive life and I would help others,"* Vandenbush said.

Although he struggled with severe injuries and post- traumatic stress disorder, he recovered and became a therapist at the Veterans Affairs Department for more than 20 years.

"People don't talk about it because they are afraid others will think they are crazy or weak. Veterans don't want to come across as being weak. But it's not weak, it's not crazy. It happens and it's important to connect with others who have experienced the same thing." Vandenbush said.

"It was then that I noticed, much to my

amazement, that most of whatever body that I was now in, was in the ground. Only my chest, shoulders, neck and head were above ground.

My friend, Ed, had died one and a half years before in a hunting accident. Yet here he was suddenly helping me out of the trench and hugging me warmly. I felt tremendous relief, love and acceptance. Tears of joy ran down both of our faces. "Hey man" he said, "I know that was rough. But you needed it, you were getting just a little bit too callous and that isn't like you. It just wasn't the Keith I knew when we played football together and hung around in high school".

I took a good look around and was in awe by the incredible beauty of the place of where we both stood. It was like a meadow with a sparkling stream running through it. The colors were much more vivid than on earth. I noticed for the first time that Ed was glowing, and I looked at my own arms and they glowed slightly too.

He said to me, "you are not doing the right thing, you should not be doing this killing.

Your mission is to help others and to protect them. You will learn more about your mission as you go along, but for now you need to go back. This is your home and you will return, but for now you need to go back and discover your mission in full." As soon as he said that I felt a pop and was instantly in pain and lying in a hospital bed."
https://www.nderf.org/Experiences/1one_soldier_nde.html

"I'd been a bit too cocky one day and almost paid the ultimate price. I was caught off guard and was taken out by a mortar shell. I floated above my body and didn't feel any pain. I couldn't believe that I could still think, see, hear and even smell. I tried to feel the pulse of my own body below me but much to my shock my fingers went through my own neck. I knew I was seriously hurt. A Corpsman I only knew as Skip showed up and I felt a sense of relief. He began calling my name and asking me if I could hear him. I suddenly was looking eye to eye with him and answering his questions although he could not hear me. I noticed that he was

bending very low over my body, yet we were eye to eye. It was then that I noticed, much to my amazement, that most of whatever body that I was now in, was in the ground. Only my chest, shoulders, neck and head were above ground.

My friend, Ed, had died one and a half years before in a hunting accident. Yet here he was suddenly helping me out of the trench and hugging me warmly. I felt tremendous relief, love and acceptance. Tears of joy ran down both of our faces. "Hey man" he said, "I know that was rough. But you needed it, you were getting just a little bit too callous and that isn't like you. It just wasn't the Keith I knew when we played football together and hung around in high school".

I took a good look around and was in awe by the incredible beauty of the place of where we both stood. It was like a meadow with a sparkling stream running through it. The colors were much more vivid than on earth. I noticed for the first time that Ed was glowing, and I looked at my own arms and they glowed slightly too.

He said to me, "you are not doing the right thing, you should not be doing this killing. Your mission is to help others and to protect them. You will learn more about your mission as you go along, but for now you need to go back. 182 *This is your home and you will return, but for now you need to go back and discover your mission in full." As soon as he said that I felt a pop and was instantly in pain and lying in a hospital bed."*
https://www.nderf.org/Experiences/1one_soldier_nde.html

—Chapter 16—
Checklist For The End Of Life

"*Oh Wow!*

Oh Wow!

Oh Wow!"

Steve Jobs

1955 - 2011

IF YOU'VE READ THIS FAR, I know you are serious about your so-called final curtain, as Frank Sinatra (1915-1988) sang in "I Did It My Way." You aren't content to wander into death unawares, as vast millions have on Earth.

You have goals. You have unmet needs and things that were never made right, which you wish were made right.

The following is a list to help you formulate your intentions still unmet. I suggest you write out your goals before you fill out your list. Your goals should make prioritizing your list easier.

People I need to forgive (even if undeserving)

People I need to ask forgiveness of:

People I owe money to:

People who owe me money (see

Unfinished tasks (the fun kind):

Unfinished tasks (perfunctory):

Unfulfilled promises to others:

Unfulfilled promises to self:

A person I need to meet:

A place I want to go:

A meal I want to try:

A book I want to read, finish, or write:

A young person I want to mentor:

An older person I want to learn from:

A charity I want to give to:

A language I'd like to learn:

An instrument I'd like to play:

A character I'd like to act out:

Something I should give away:

A gift I need to give someone:

A gift I need to give to myself:

Teacher(s) I need to thank:

A deity I need to praise and thank:

(Please extend this list with whatever will inspire you to take action on your own behalf)

Hopefully, you can fill the list out before you finish and set aside this book. We tend to desire the ideal closure to our life; a sense that we've fulfilled our destiny. Don't let your to-do list become a barrier to closure; instead, make the list a guidepost to closure. Give yourself the grace to not have to get each one done to feel fulfilled. Perhaps when your #1 item gets done, maybe even #2 and #3, you can decide you have accomplished what you set out to do. Then, let all the others just be icing on the cake. Do what you can while you can with the resources you have.

—Chapter 17—
You Can't Take It With You

"The man who dies rich, dies disgraced."
Andrew Carnegie
1835 - 1919

This book isn't intended to focus on any-one's finances, but Carnegie's words are a modern proverb we can't ignore. Some of you may be old enough to remember the consummate comedian Bob Hope (1903-2003). One of his favorite lines was: *"You heard the saying: 'You can't take it with you?' Well, I saw Jack Benny coming out of a store the other day with an asbestos suitcase."* That line always made folks laugh. But it's time to seriously consider that axiom, plus Carnegie's quote, and how they affect us.

If you are too young to know of Andrew

Carnegie, the significance of what he believed won't germinate in your mind. So, let's just say he was the Warren Buffet (1930-) or Bill Gates (1955-) of his day. Carnegie came to the United States at the age of thirteen as a legal immigrant. He learned English and yearned to read books, but his folks were too poor to afford them. As a youngster, a friend introduced him to a wealthy neighbor named Colonel James Anderson (1785- 1861). Anderson had a library and freely lent books out to working boys, including wide-eyed Andrew. In Carnegie's words: *"The windows were opened in the walls of my dungeon through which the light of knowledge streamed in."*

That moment not only opened the world of reading to the boy but also set him on a course of learning new skills. The seminal skill I remember he learned was Morse Code. To communicate by telegraph with a series of dots and dashes in 1839 was tantamount to being an IT tech or network administrator. Having learned this high-tech skill, he got a good job with the railroad.

His railroad gig put him in contact with the biggest movers and shakers in America (in both government and private industry). These exposures to great minds, risk-takers, negotiators, and brave men of integrity formed who Carnegie came to be. With his key position came key contacts and opportunity. With the seizing of opportunity came advancement. Upon receiving a credible stock tip, Carnegie and his wife bought ten shares of Adams Express Company and did quite well. Later, he purchased Woodruff Sleeping Car Company, then another business, and parlayed the game of mergers and acquisitions to amass a fortune in the steel business and collateral interests in mining, ships, railroads, and oil wells. In 1901, his estimated net worth was $490 million. In that era, he was certifiably "filthy rich." During his formative years, he learned that vast riches can complement a man or ruin a man. Drawing from the highest integrity observed from his railroad days with the power brokers as a youth, he purposed to own and dispose his money and not let it own and dispose him.

Recalling Anderson's kindness in lending Carnegie books, he was bent to do the same on a much grander scale. To Carnegie, access to books was not a right but a privilege. Why not extend the privilege he had to others in his former situation? Thus, he literally pioneered the free lending library movement in America by donating millions of dollars to cities and small towns to fund over two thousand libraries, so that the youngsters that took the initiative to read would have materials to read and learn from. They could read about foreign places they could never travel to; they could learn a new language or a skill; they could learn history and its lessons as time marches on. In short, they could dream dreams unimaginable to non-readers. With those dreams came a new level of freedom, not the freedom that emanates from the accumulation of money but the freedom that emanates from the accumulation of knowledge. Before Andrew Carnegie died on August 11,1919, he made a huge difference to millions of Americans. Nearly one hundred years after his death, we are still benefitting from his generosity ... his vision. Through what began as his philanthropy, kids in the twenty-first century have Sesame Street, and college students have access to Pell Grants, both to further their educations. What can regular folks, like us, learn from this man? I call it the Carnegie Principle, and it should fit in with your end-of-earthly-life goals and mine. When he gained the resources, this scruffy, Scottish immigrant purposed to not die in disgrace. That is an achievement I think we can all wrap our minds around, but what lies ahead for us? Well, to begin with, our lives should not reflect the old adage *"Get all you can, can all you get, and sit on the can."* No, that is a perverse amalgamation of fear and egocentrism.

The account balance of your IRA or 401(k) will not be engraved on your tombstone. Neither will the market value of any stocks you owned the day your body died. The keys to your car, boat, or RV—your pride and joy—will not be there either. It's safe to say you'll have no need of those things then, but others (remaining) still have needs. Whether they are books or clothes or housing or transportation or education or a trade or decent food, those needs are out there. I see the Carnegie Principle as investing in things that can have long- lasting, even eternal, dividends. That means distribution to people. The choices are many: from educational scholarships, to child sponsorship, to angel-funding or micro loans for a new business (someone else's dream).

People who brag about the money and resources they give away reveal they haven't made the effort to connect with the gratitude of the recipients and those around them. But even if you are affecting those in faraway countries, you rest in the knowledge that their world is a better place because you followed the Carnegie Principle; because you reached out; because you cared. That, in and of itself, is reward enough.

There are many opportunities for you to invest in people and causes that will outlive your body on Earth. To die having given so much as to be personally vulnerable is to die a wise person... one who leaves this world not with debts and liabilities but with targeted resources and assets fit to bless others. This is a remonstrance that I have taken to heart, and I know you can too.

"Those who report meeting a divine being generally portray God as someone who radiates incredible love, light, grace, and acceptance. This is not religious dogma or theology, but one of the most consistent claims of multiple individuals who have encountered a heavenly being."

"... people are not merely stating or projecting their religious yearnings or beliefs, but, like the explorers of old, are describing an entity they have encountered. The fact that they describe these encounters so similarly gives us confidence that they have, indeed, met the same Being."

Dr. Jeffrey Long

I close this book with a poem a friend of mine wrote. It is about our final dream. The Irish-descent relative he wrote it for had died in his sleep.

—Chapter 18—

Final Dream

"If you are graced to leave
The surely bonds of life
Upon the wings of dreams
Away from earthly strife

Then there will come a dream
That will be your very last
A thought that reigns supreme
While you're sleeping fast.

We cannot know that dream
That you will ride upon
Beyond the setting sun
Before the misty dawn.

Perhaps 'twill be a meal
You wish would always last
With perfect company
A very grand repast.

Perhaps 'twill be a look
Across the waters still

With bait upon the hook
To catch the gleaming gill.

Life can be a race.
An Irish proverb tells
It's not the strain of running
But that you finish well.

If life's an open book
A gift... a true godsend.
Then like a book or poem
Comes time to say:
THE END."

Are you prepared for the end? By now,
you should be at peace with where
you go from here.
May your conclusion be accurate and
lead to uninterrupted happiness.

"When the panoramic life review ended,
despite the many obvious mistakes I had
made in my life, I experienced no retribution
– no judgment and no punishment. I was the
only judge presiding over my day in court!

Given time to assimilate my life in retrospect, I was given the opportunity to know, firsthand, both the happiness and the sorrow I had created through my actions. I came to the realization that, more often than not, I had lived in a devastatingly selfish manner. My heart was filled with shame and remorse. The impact of that emotional avalanche remains uppermost in my mind to this very day.

However, after my time of reflection in the Heavens that day, the Being of Light telepathically conveyed these words: Who you are is the difference that God makes, and the difference is love.

Dannion

Appendix/Resources

Very few Veterans share their NDE stories, just as many are reluctant to say anything at all about any of their combat experiences. Bottling up these emotions and memories is a big part of the survival struggle Veterans face every day of their lives. That's what makes the following two stories very special, and also why I'm putting them here at the end of the book, so that they can stand out in their courage and insight. I have not changed their language – it is the rough voice of combat veterans, undiluted by political correctness.

Sam's Story

"I don't know what was in that last spike but it was some evil shit and the last thing I remember was a couple of a**holes rolling me over, going through my pockets and then stealing my shoes. I could see them doing it but couldn't move or say anything. The bastards rolled and robbed me while I lay

there with that hypo in my arm and I knew I was dying but I didn't actually give a sh*t. Two tours in Iraq, a couple of medals, and then nothing – no job, no friends, no family and nobody home for me. I went on the streets and never looked back. I remember I was actually happy to finally be dying.

But I don't remember dying – it just seemed like one minute I was looking up at those ugly aces and then the next minute wham – I was walking through the streets of a village and I thought "Damn. How did I get here"? I knew I was back in Iraq. I looked down, saw that I wasn't geared up and had no weapon, and started to get worried. Then I came around a corner and there was Jack with that big stupid grin on his face. Problem was, the last time I had seen Jack he was in little pieces all over the road after the IED took out his Humvee. Now there he was, all in one piece and then by God he walked up and put his arms around me.
I was in the light. I said "Is this heaven? Am I dead? Who are they?" "You're dead

206

old buddy, but this isn't heaven", Jack said. Then he waved at the people in the shadows and they began to gather around. "But it's not your time yet and I'm here to tell you that all these people you killed forgive you and now you have to go back and get your shit together and do what you were sent to do in the first place."

"What do you mean?" I said. "What am I supposed to do?" I started to feel a little dizzy and reached out to hold on to Jack but he started to fade, and the people in the shadows raised their hands like a blessing of some kind and then I felt myself slipping and falling and I felt like it was lasting forever. Then I woke up – that's all I can say; I woke up even though I hadn't been asleep, with a couple of cops standing over me. When they saw me looking up at them one of them said "Hey look – this a**hole's been DOA for five minutes and now he's awake. How the f**k did that happen." His partner bent over me and took my pulse and said "F**k if I know

but this guy's alive."

F**k if I knew either, but I realized right away that I felt amazing. Lying there in that alley, DOA as far as anyone knew, evil sh*t running through my body and yet – I suddenly felt great! I sat up. "Whoa there buddy" one of the cops said. "Just lie still and we'll get you help." I couldn't talk so I just nodded, but I knew that I was going to be OK. They took me to the ER, and then I was checked in to the VA for a couple of weeks and began my program. I had been through detox before but this time was different. I felt different, not like I was going to have to give something up but like I was working on something new and even hopeful.

As it turns out that's what happened. Believe it or not I'm now a drug and alcohol counselor working with Vets who are in the same kind of deep sh*t that was swallowing me before I died and had my meeting with Jack and the people in the shadows. I don't know for sure where I was but I know that, according to the cops, I had been dead and *gone and then I was back. I think I'm finding out what Jack meant, and I really do feel like I'm doing what I was sent to do. I'm saving lives now, and I hope I'm getting right with all those people in the shadows who forgave me for what I did to them back in that other life. That's how I think of it – my other life. I feel like I've been given a second chance, but damned if I know what I ever did to deserve this. But I'll take it, and thank whatever God there is who gave it to me. I hope I'm getting it right this time. I'm working at it."*

Pedro's Story

"I saw the incoming just before it hit. We were flying low over the Delta and started taking fire from the village. We had turned to go back for a firing pass and the NVA stepped out of a hooch and let loose on us before we could react. I saw the flash and felt a quick pressure, like somebody shoving me and then nothing. I came to lying on a trail in the jungle and started feeling around to see if all my parts were there. Everything seemed fine and I figured I must have been

209

*blown out of the chopper and somehow
landed OK, so I got up and started walking.
It seemed a little strange – not a sound, no
smells, a funny kind of light all around me
and I couldn't feel the usual heat and
humidity. I came around a bend in the path
and there in front of me grinning were Big
Dave and Slim Jim, both guys I had been
real close to all through my first tour in
'Nam. Problem was – they were dead. Killed
in an NVA mortar attack over a year back,
just as we were all wrapping up our time in-
country. I know because I helped pull what
was left of them together and put them in
body bags.*

*"What the f**k!" I whispered to myself. I
knew something wasn't right. "Hey troop,
how's it hanging?" Big Dave said way too
loudly. That startled me - "Hey man, keep it
down! NVA are all over this goddamned
place. What are you doing here anyway?"
Slim Jim walked right up to me, put his hand
on my shoulder, and said "Hey Man, the
question is what are you doing here. It's not
your time."*

That got to me. "Not my time? What the f**k do you mean, and where are we. You're both dead!"

"Yeah, we're dead" Big Dave said, "but you're not. Not yet anyway." Things got a little crazy then – I had a lot of questions, but they just stood there shaking their heads. "Hey man – orders came down and you have to go back. That's it." They stepped back and saluted and then poof – they were gone and I was lying in smoking bloody wreckage in a rice paddy looking up at the medevac chopper just overhead coming down to get me. I passed out then and came to back in Danang at the 8th Field Hospital where they gave me a temporary patching up and sent me on to Okinawa where I stayed for five weeks before I shipped out stateside.

To this day I wonder what happened over there and whether I was just hallucinating or if I really saw Big Dave and Slim Jim over on the other side and then came back. All I know if that my life changed after that – I came back from Nam a different guy than the one who went there, and I've found a more peaceful life. I'm a Christian minister and spend my time working with homeless Vets and others who have lost their way. I don't know if I've found the way or not, but I do believe that what happened, happened. I have a faith now that I can't explain – it just seemed to settle on me while I was in the hospital in Okinawa, and ever since I've had a feeling that being sent back was for real and that I have a real purpose in life."

RESOURCES FOR BATTLING ADDICTIONS AND DESTRUCTIVE BEHAVIORS

The following self-help venues are offered as a starting point to aid you in finding useful tools to overcome life's challenges. Organizations listed are not to be construed as my endorsement or dissemination of any kind of medical advice.

*"After a series of paranormal events like the one I had with my sister, the last pillar of my atheism toppled. It took 21 years for me to fully align with what I experienced during my near-death experience. In the end, two organizations saved the day: The **International Association for Near- Death Studies** (IANDS) and **Alcoholics Anonymous** (AA). These two organizations helped me reach the point where I could tell God that I loved It and promised I would never turn away again — and I haven't."*

Louisa Peck

ALCOHOL

213

Alcoholics Anonymous
https://www. aa. org/
"An international fellowship of men and women who have had a drinking problem. It is nonprofessional, self-supporting, multi- racial, apolitical, and available almost everywhere."

American Addiction Centers
https://americanaddictioncenters.org/ Alcoholism-treatment/support/
"Our mission is to provide quality, compassionate, and innovative care to adults struggling with addiction and co-occurring mental health disorders."

Substance Abuse and Mental Health Services (SAMSHA)
https://www.samhsa.gov/find-help/national-helpline
SAMHSA's National Helpline, 1-800-662-HELP (4357), is a confidential, free, 24-hour-a- day, 365-day-a-year, information service, in English and Spanish, for individuals and

family members facing mental and/or substance use disorders."

National Institute on Alcohol Abuse and Alcoholism
https://pubs.niaaa.nih.gov/
"NIAAA supports and conducts research on the impact of alcohol use on human health and well-being. It is the largest funder of alcohol research in the world."

DEPRESSION
Anxiety and Depression Association of America (ADAA)
https://adaa.org
"An international non-profit dedicated to the prevention, treatment, & cure of anxiety, depression, and related disorders."

Depression and Bipolar Support Alliance (DBSA)
http://WWW.dbsalliance. org/
"Providing hope, help, support, and

215

education to improve the lives of people who have mood disorders."

Families for Depression Awareness
http://www.familyaware. org
"[We] help families recognize and cope with depression and bipolar disorder to get people well and prevent suicides."

DRUGS
Teen Challenge
www. teenchallengeusa. com
"We endeavor to help people become mentally sound, emotionally balanced, socially adjusted, physically well, and spiritually alive."

National Institute on Drug Abuse (NIH)
www.drugahuse.gov/patients-families
"Our mission is to advance science on the causes and consequences of drug use and addiction and to apply that knowledge to improve individual and public health." A portal for treatment sources, this site supplies helpful articles for teens, adults, and families.

Narcotics Anonymous (NA)

WWW. na. org/meetingsearch

"A nonprofit... society of men and women for whom drugs had become a major problem. We are recovering addicts who meet regularly to help each other stay clean."

EATING DISORDERS

National Eating Disorders Association (NEDA)

www. nationaleatingdisorders. org "A national non-profit that supports individuals and families affected by eating disorders, and

serves as a catalyst for prevention, cures and access to quality care."

FEAR, ANXIETY, AND STRESS

Be In Health

www.beinhealth.com

"Discover healing in God for your spirit, soul, and body."

GAMBLING

Gamblers Anonymous

www.gamblersanonymous. org
"A fellowship of men and women who share their experience, strength and hope with each other that they may solve their common problem and help others to recover from a gambling problem."

SELF-MUTILATION
Self-Injury Outreach & Support
http://sioutreach. org
"Providing information and resources about self-injury to those who self-injure, those who have recovered, and those who want to help"
S.A.EE Alternatives (Self-Abuse Finally Ends) https://selfinjury, com/
"Committed to helping you and others achieve an end to self- injurious behavior."
Self-Mutilators Anonymous
www.selfmutilatorsanonymous. org
"A fellowship of men and women who share their experience, strength, and hope with each other, that they may

solve their common problem and help others to recover from physical self-mutilation."

POST-TRAUMATIC STRESS DISORDER
PTSD Alliance
www.ptsdalliance.org
"Five national and international organizations— here to serve individuals with Posttraumatic Stress Disorder."

Combat Stress [UK]
www. combatstress. org. uk
"Helping former servicemen and women deal with issues like trauma, anxiety, depression, and post-traumatic stress disorder."

Mission 22
www.mission22. com/#ourcause
"Full Spectrum Health and Mission 22 have developed a personalized, whole person approach to healing veterans."

Operation We Are Here

www.opemtionwearehere.com/PTSD.ht
m l

"We are a non-denominational ministry
providing a comprehensive list of
resources for the military community
and its supporters."

PTSD Foundation of America

http://ptsdusa.org/about-us/our-mission/

"A non-profit organization dedicated to
mentoring to our combat veterans and
their families with post-traumatic
stress."

Point Man Ministries (PMIM)

www.pmim.org

"Run by veterans from all conflicts,
nationalities and backgrounds ... the
primary focus of Point Man has always
been to offer spiritual healing from
PTSD."

GENDER DYSPHORIA

The Center

https://gaycenter. org

"Where everyone is celebrated for who

they are. The Center... provid[es] programs for health, wellness and community connection."

Restored Hope Network
WWW. restoredhopenetwork. org "An inter-denominational membership governed network
dedicated to restoring hope to those broken by sexual and relational sin, especially those impacted by homosexuality.
Journey Canada
www.journeycanada.org
"A community-based, Christ- centered discipleship ministry that exists to help people find hope and live life through experiencing Jesus in their relationships, sexuality and identity."

Pure Life Ministries
www.purelifeministries. org
"PLM offers help to Christians touched by same- sex attractions."
SEX ADDICTIONS

Sex Addicts Anonymous
https://saa-recovery. org
"A fellowship of men and women who share their experience, strength and hope with each other, so they may overcome their sexual addiction and help others recover."
Pure Life Ministries
wwwpurelifeministries. org "Whether you are ensnared in internet, pornography ... or involved in some other form of
illicit sexual behavior, you've come to the right place."

Pure Desire Ministries
https://puredesire. org
"For men, women, and students who are searching for hope, freedom, and healing from the pain of sexual addiction, intimacy disorders, betrayal, and shame."

XXX Church
www.xxxchurch. com

Christian-based organization that "help[s] men and women who are struggling with porn online - break secret habits, crush shame, and create a great life with a healthy view of sex through our online community and resources."

SUICIDE
National Suicide Prevention Lifeline
https://suicidepreventionlifeline.org 1 (800) 273-8255
"NSPL provides 24/7, free and confidential support for people in distress, prevention and crisis resources for you or your loved ones."
Christian Suicide Prevention
www.christiansuicideprevention. com
"Committed to saving the lives of Christians and non-Christians alike by educating and empowering people through Biblical principles to understand the grace of God and their God-given authority over all adverse situations and circumstances; through a

professional crisis phone line and e- mail service."

https://www.ncbi.nlm.nih.gov/pubmed/ 3 961880
"Attempted suicide is correlated with an increase subsequent risk of committed suicide. However, preliminary data and psychodynamic hypotheses suggest that serious suicide attempts followed by transcendental near-death experiences (NDEs) may decrease rather than increase subsequent overt suicide risk, despite the NDEs' apparent "romanticization" of death."

References & Useful Research
Greyson, B. Near-death encounters with and without near-death experiences: comparative NDE scale profiles. J Near Death Stud.1990;8:151–161

Parnia, S., Waller, D.G., Yeates, R., and Fenwick, P. A qualitative and quantitative study of the incidence, features and etiology of near-death experiences in cardiac arrest survivors. Resuscitation.2001;48:149–156

Shushan, G. Conceptions of the afterlife in early civilizations: universalism, constructivism and near-death experience. Continuum, New York/London; 2009
Veterans NDE Resources
A wide variety of NDE resources for combat veterans and their families

https://iands.org/resources/support/com b at-veterans.html

Good video discussion of NDEs, Military Issues and Veterans' experiences from the 2016 IANDS Conference. https://www.youtube.com/watch?v=vAe 2P SmYQ7Y

A good podcast discussion of "The Combat Veteran NDE Project" with the

founder.
https://www.talkzone.com/episodes/204/
NDE012014.html

Principal Combat NDE Research Study
Sullivan, R. M., "Combat-related near-
death experiences: a preliminary
investigation", Anabiosis: J Near Death
Studies, 1984;4(2):143–52

Chapter References

Chapter 3
Excerpts from Out on a Broken Limb
(Eugene, OR: Harvest House Publishers,
1985) used by permission of the author,
F. LaGard Smith.
The Clearing:
https://www.theclearingnw.com/

Chapter 7
Movie death counts:
https://www.gocompare.com/ life-
insurance/ directors-cut/.

Chapter 9
Excellent study of 154 patients:
https://www.frontiersin.org/
journals/human-neuroscience.

Ten accounts of near-death experiences
from the Near-Death Experience
Research Foundation Studies (NDERF).
All rights reserved. Reprinted with
respect to NDERF policy for commercial

educational materials and Fair Use Doctrine. These accounts, in their entirety, are freely available via NDERF internet archive, http://www.nderf.org.

Taylor NDE #8434:
https://tinyurl.com/ygevsg4x
Keith NDE #8435:
https://tinyurl.com/yeh7ck9u

Richard NDE #8403:
https://tinyurl.com/yhoe9tfy
James NDE #8383:
https://tinyurl.com/ykxnsze6
Missy NDE #8330:
https://tinyurl.com/yfzj2gkj

Patricia NDE #8371:
https://tinyurl.com/yjc4cduj
Alejandra NDE #8357:
https://tinyurl.com/yfl2a2ed
Heidi NDE #8354:
https://tinyurl.com/yfeolxr8
Dean NDE #8346:
https://tinyurl.com/yjdlpj2a

Zdenka FDE #23235:
https://tinyurl.com/yegp2fen

Do you have a near death experience to share? Go to
http://www.nderf.org/ShareNDE.html
AWARE study:
http://www.horizonresearch.org/
Uploads/Journal_Resuscitation 2_.pdf

Chapter 10
Quote sources: Goodreads,
https://www.goodreads. com/quotes/
Brainy Quote, https://www.
brainyquote.com/.

Chapter 11
Dr. Weiss info:
http://www.brianweiss.com/
Dr. Stevenson info:
https://med.virginia.edu/ perceptual-
studies/who-we-are/dr-ian-stevenson/

Chapter 13

Ages and longevity of celebrities:
http://www. deadoraliveinfo.com/

Chapter 14
Lucas Medal of Honor citation:
https://tinyurl.com/ygrtle3v

Doss Medal of Honor citation:
https://tinyurl.com/yz7epakf

About the Author

Leroy Nelson was born on January of 1935, in Longview, Washington. He graduated from Western Washington University in 1958, receiving a BA in education. Leroy taught school in Battleground, Washington, and then LaCenter, Washington. Because of his lifelong passion for sports he coached boy's football, basketball, and baseball. In 1966, Nelson earned a Master of Science in counseling and guidance from Portland State University.

Involved in business ventures throughout his life, Leroy's lasting accomplishment came with the opening of Columbia River Floor Covering in 1966. He officially retired in 2000. Following the Carnegie Principle, Nelson and his wife fund educational scholarships for selected Longview, Washington, high school seniors.

Made in the USA
Columbia, SC
06 March 2020

88610223R00126